D1167904

The
Best
FREE
THINGS
in America

by Linda & Bob Kalian

Library of Congress Cataloging-in-Publication Data
Kalian, Robert
Kalian, Linda

The Best Free Things In America

ISBN 0-934968-11-X

1. Consumer Reference   2. Catalog Free Things

Quantity discounts are available. Teachers, fund raisers, premium users,
write to us at the address below regarding the quantities needed.

Publisher: Roblin Press, 405 Tarrytown Road Suite 414,White Plains, NY 10607
(914) 347-6671   Fax: (914) 592-1167

CONTENTS

Something For Everyone 7

Music 28

Crafts & Hobbies 29

For Pet Lovers.. 35

Cookbooks 38

Home & Garden 57

Stay Healthy 69

For Kids 87

Religion 91

Special Free Offers 94

Learning Can Be Fun 95

College & Beyond.. 103

Looking Good 107

Computers 109

Conservation 112

For Sports Fans 113

Car & Drivers... 122

Travel.. 126

Traveling The USA 128

Foreign Travel.. 135

Money Matters 142

Free From The U.S. Government 149

Consumer Information From The U.S. Government .. 153

Free Groceries & Gifts... 174

A Few Words Before We Start

You're about to embark on a fascinating journey, the journey to the world of FREE THINGS. Most people have no idea just how many fantastic things are waiting for them free for the asking. Before you begin, read the few tips we've included below.

1. Save money - use a postcard whenever possible (unless they request a SASE or a nominal shipping charge – (there aren't many of these).

2. SASE — means send a long (#10) self-addressed stamped envelope. Your freebee will be returned to you in your own envelope.

3. Be sure to include your ZIP CODE - Without it you may never receive your gift (since many items are sent to you via third class mail).

4. Ask for the items you want by name. Often companies will have several gifts available and won't know which one you're asking for unless you specify.

5. Teachers, civic and religious groups: If you'd like quantities of any item, ask for it and mention what it's for. Usually you'll get the quantity you need.

6. If you use a product or have any favorable comment to make, the companies appreciate hearing about it. Many of these freebies are part of a company's efforts to get you to know...and hopefully like...their products. They appreciate a kind word (don't we all.)

7. Be patient. Some gifts may start coming within a week or two but others take longer - often a month or even more. The reason is that companies are often flooded with requests and it takes time to process them.

8. There's a lot here. Don't try to send for everything at one or two sittings. Start with the sections that interest you most.

9. Every item was available at the time the book was written. However, sometimes supplies of an item may run out and the offer may be withdrawn or replaced with a new freebie. (Please let us know at the addess below if you come across any of these so we can update the next edition of this book...thanks)

10. Have Fun!

Roblin Press
Dept BFT-97
PO Box 125
Hartsdale, NY 10530

Something For Everyone

Free For The Asking – Right In Your Own Back Yard

The first thing to remember is that there are lots of things all around you that are free for the asking. All you have to do is be aware of them and to *ASK*. Here are just a few examples:

FREE PETS

Your local paper may have ads for free kittens and pups when their cats have litters and dogs have pups. Animal shelters also have free pets. Most often they will only ask you to pay for the shots.

FREE LAND FILL/FIRE WOOD

Some contractors offer free land fill and free top soil when they want to get rid of it. The only catch might be that you have to remove it (or pay a nominal delivery charge.) Check out construction sites. You can often get free fire wood when they are clearing the land.

FREE COMPUTER SERVICES

There are tons of offers to try different things before you buy. For example computer online services offer a variety of free trials just to get you to try their service or to surf the Internet. Call:

AMERICA ON LINE (CURRENTLY OFFERING **50** FREE HOURS JUST FOR SIGNING ON): **1-888-265-8002**
PRODIGY: **1-800-776-3449**
COMPUSERVE: **1-800-848-8990**

LOOKING GOOD

Free haircuts are available through some of your local beauty and barber schools. Check your phone book and give them a call. Some may ask a small fee or a tip for the trainee. Some of your larger hair designers may offer free style and cuts

certain months or certain times of the year. Call your favorite salon and find out when they are training their students. You benefit by getting the designer him/herself for free. (In their salon they may charge anywhere from $50.00 and up.) Companies like Clairol often offer free hair coloring when they are testing new products. Don't hesitate to give any of them a call. Remember, if you don't ask you'll never know.

Want to try free perfume or have a makeover? Try any one of your larger department stores. You are never obligated to buy and some of the companies will even give you free product samples. You could have a ball going from store to store. Next time you need a new look, try your local department store.

FREE FOR CONSUMERS

Supermarket bulletin boards offer free items that neighbors may want to get rid of or trade.

Credit card companies offer free month trials on discount shopping clubs, travel, insurance and offer all kinds of specials. The one thing you have to remember is if you don't want it, after the month is up, cancel it.

You can even get free magazine subscriptions, tapes and CD's just for asking. Always remember to look in your local paper for deals at the supermarkets for buy one item, get one free.

FREE TRAVEL

There are lots of options around for free or almost free travel. If you have a unique specialty, many cruise lines will give you a free trip when you give a lecture about your specialty on one of their cruises. They often have theme cruises you might fit in with. For example, if you are a fitness specialist they often look for people to teach aerobics on board. So if you have a special skill, the cruise line might feel it is special enough to give you a free trip if you spend a few hours instructing others while on the cruise. Check the toll-free directory for the phone numbers of the cruise lines.

There are some courier services that will ask you to carry a package anywhere in the world they travel to. With that you get a free trip for carrying the parcel. Sometimes you can get to stay a few extra days as long as you can catch their plane on the return flight.

The airlines still offer you free tickets (sometimes anywhere they fly in the world) for changing your flight if they are overbooked. So think twice the next time they ask if you would consider taking a later flight. Frequent flyer fares are still a good deal as long as they are offered. Make sure you are a member of the frequent flyer club if you plan on doing any airline travel. They usually don't put a time restriction on them.

When they travel, some families look for housesitters. In return for watching their home, you get a free place to live. If you like to travel, you can might even trade apartments and homes with people in other parts of the country (or the world) through different real estate exchanges. Check the classified section of your local newspaper.

FREE FOR USING YOUR CREDIT CARD

The credit card war is heating up...and you stand to benefit. Today more and more banks and companies are offering credit cards that come with added bonuses for using it. For example, some banks offer credit cards that give you one frequent flyer mile for each dollar you charge on their card. You can use the miles to get free airline tickets. Also, many larger chain stores offer you free dollars to spend in their store just for opening a charge account with them. There is no obligation to use the card and you can cut it up if you don't plan to use it.

FREE DINNER

Don't forget that there are quite a few restaurant chains that offer you a free dinner on your birthday. All you have to show is a license or some proof of your birthdate.

Also check the ads for local restaurants that offer those great coupons for buy-one dinner get-one free.

FREE LONG DISTANCE CALLS

Because of all the competition with phone companies, if you are willing to switch they will offer you all kinds of deals from $100.00 checks to several hours of free calls. Shop around for the best deal before you sign up with another phone company.

FREE ENTERTAINMENT

Don't overlook all the free concerts and theatre productions in all community parks outdoors especially in the summer months. Check with your local parks and recreation department.

Many local movie theatres have deals on slow nights. Our local movie theatre offers a special on Tuesday nights: Buy one ticket, get one free. Check it out.

If you like concerts and drama some theatre and opera companies offer ushers (if you are willing to work a shift) free tickets in exchange for your work.

These are just a small handful of the tons of free and practically free offers all around you all the time. The important thing is to keep an eye out for them and take advantage of them where they are of interest to you.

ELDERCARE BY PHONE

Getting help and information about services for older people anywhere in the United States is now possible. There is a new national *"Eldercare Locator"* service. Dial: **1-800-677-1116** between 9 a.m. and 5p.m. Monday through Friday. Have the name and address of the person to be assisted, the zip code and a brief description of the service or information needed. The "Eldercare Locator" provides information about adult day -care centers, legal assistance, home health services and more. This service taps into a nationwide network of organizations familiar with state and local community services throughout the country.

SWEET BREATH

Did you know that eating parsley keeps your breath fresh? Well instead of going around with a spray of parsley hanging from your mouth, you can have the next best thing, BreathAsure™. BreathAsure™ is sunflower oil and parsley seed oil in a soft gelatin shell. BreathAsure™ is the all natural "Internal Breath Freshener®," send a self-addressed stamped envelope to:

BREATHASURE, INC.
FREE SAMPLE
26115 MUREAU ROAD
CALABASS, CA 91302-3126

BOOK BARGAINS

"Catalog of Book Bargains" is for all book lovers that want to save 90% or more off original prices. Some recent best sellers are included in this 50 page catalog. Free from:

P. DAEDALUS BOOKS INC.
BOX 9132
HYATTSVILLE, MD. 20781
OR CALL: 1-800-395-2665

BACK TALK

Back talk and how to deal with it constructively is some handy advice Covenant House offers you for dealing with your child. These helpful tips will open lines of communication and help keep you in touch with your child before he/she gets out of hand. If you need expert advice or support their NINELINE at 1-800-999-9999. They will put you in touch with people who can help you right in your own town.

GET RICH AT HOME

Have you ever dreamed of starting your own business from your home? If so you will want to get the *Mail Order Success Secrets report*. Learn how to start in your spare time with little money and grow rich in the most exciting business in the world. Send a SASE to:

ROBLIN-BFT
405 TARRYTOWN RD. SUITE 414
WHITE PLAINS, NY 10607

FRESH BREATH

These great *Fresh Breath Capsules* will help you cure your bad breath internally. Dont worry...the next time you eat garlic or spicy food, pop one of these Breath Fresh capsules. They also have other great products like Retinol A, Ultramins plus Vitamins and Thigh Cream. To try the Breath Freshener, send $1.00 to cover postage and handling to:

21ST CENTURY GROUP
10 CHESTNUT STREET
SPRING VALLEY, NY 10877

"THE GOOD LIFE CATALOG"

If you are a cigar smoker or know someone who is, this catalog is a must. Not only will you find every cigar you can think of, but all the accessories that go with them. There is a 'Cigar Hall of Fame"and even some unusual and interesting gifts for people who don't smoke. Drop a card to:

THE THOMPSON COMPANY
5401 HANGAR COURT
P.O. BOX 30303
TAMPA, FL 33630-3303

SURPRISE GIFT CLUB

We've all faced the problem of what to give someone as a gift. Finally there's help. The Surprise Gift of the Month Club has developed an innovative solution. They will offer you a broad selection of items from kites, iron ons, coasters, stickers, records, crewel and needlepoint kits and many more items to select from. Anyone young or old will be delighted to receive a gift each month. It's a nice way to say "I'm thinking of you" to someone special. For a sample of the assorted crewel and needlepoint kits, send $1.00 for postage and handling to:

SURPRISE GIFT OF THE MONTH CLUB
55 RAILROAD AVE.
GARNERVILLE, NY 10923

BEST FOOT FORWARD

When your feet ache and you are looking for some kind of relief what can you do? The Podi-

atric Association of America has a toll-free number you can call to get assistance. Call:
1-800-FOOT-CARE

ELDERHOSTEL
Elderhostel offers moderately priced learning vacations across the United States and Canada as well as 45 nations abroad for senior citizens who enjoy adventure and travel but who have a limited amount of money to spend. The subjects taught on these vacations range from astronomy, to zoology. For a catalog of courses and travel iteneraries, write:
ELDERHOSTEL
75 FEDERAL ST., THIRD FLOOR
BOSTON, MA. 02110-1941
OR CALL **1-617-426-7788**

PARENTS WITH YOUNG CHILDREN
If you plan to have a child or have one already, you might find *"Financial Strategies for New Parents"* to be helpful. This freebie from the International Association for Financial Planning, helps you prepare for parenthood. It includes a list of 10 things to do, such as setting goals, looking at your cash flow, making a will, talking to your employer about company benefits to determine if you have enough insurance. For a free copy, call the Association at:
1-800-945-IAFP

HOUSE OF ONYX
If you like gems and gemstones...whether in the rough or finished into fine jewelry or artifacts, this catalog is for you. You will find some fabulous closeout buys on some fantastic gemstones, geodes even Mexican onyx and malachite carvings. If you are just a collector or need some great gifts send for this catalog. Write:
HOUSE OF ONYX
THE AARON BUILDING
120 MAIN ST.
GREENVILLE, KY 42345

HOME BUYING

Are you considering buying a house? This 160 page book from Lawyers Title Insurance Corp. is a must for you. It will help answer all those questions you have about owning your own home. Ask for The Process of Home Buying. Send 75¢ postage & handling to:
LAWYERS TITLE INSURANCE CORP.
DEPT. CW
6630 WEST BROAD ST.
BOX 27567
RICHMOND, VA 23230

CONSUMER GEM KIT

Buying a valuable gem can be a tricky affair unless you are prepared. Have you ever wondered what makes one diamond more valuable than another that may look the same to the naked eye? Before buying any gemstone it is essential to learn exactly what to look for. For example do you know the 4 'C's' that determine a diamond's value? They are... Cut... Color... Clarity... Carat (weight). To learn more about what to look for when buying a diamond, send for a free consumer kit from the American Gem Society. Send a card to:
THE AMERICAN GEM SOCIETY
8881 W. SAHARA AVE.
LAS VEGAS, NV 89117

SLEEP TIGHT

A healthful good night's sleep makes for a very productive, pleasant person. Learn all the facts on how to get a healthful sleep, by selecting the right bedding pillows and positions. The makers of Simmons will send you this free book *"Consumer Guide To Better Sleep"* plus several others including *It's Never Too Early To Start Caring For Your Back* and tips for shopping for the right bed. Send a business-sized SASE to:
SIMMONS BEAUTYREST
ONE CONCOURSE CENTER, SUITE 600
BOX C-93
ATLANTA, GA 30328

KNIFE SHOWPLACE

This catalog with hundreds of knives, swords specialty and novelty knives, sharpening systems, accessories , etc. will help you find that special carving knife for apples, cheese or fruitcake. If you are a collector of swords and sheaths there are a few to choose from. Write:

SMOKY MOUNTAIN KNIFE WORKS
BOX 4430
SEVIERVILLE, TN 37864

SHIRT BUCKLES

Give your clothes some style with these solid color shirt buckles. They come in an assortment of colors. Send SASE plus 25¢ for one buckle and 25¢ for each additional one to:

THE GIFT BOX
193 E. M-35
PO BOX 1237
GWINN, MI 49841

HAPPY CHILD - HAPPY ADULT

Parenting is difficult. Sometimes you need to take a few minutes to calm down before disciplining your child. Next time you feel like hitting your child, try another approach. For example you might do something like making an origami paper hat, or any game that gives you the time you need to cool off. Remember the time it takes to make a paper hat could keep you from hurting your child. For this excellent free book write:

"PREVENTING CHILD ABUSE"
PO BOX 2866 P
CHICAGO, IL 60690

THE POSITIVE PROSPECTOR

Everything we seem to hear on the television, news, radio and through the newspapers is negative. Isn't it time for a little good news? "The Positive Prospector will send you a free copy of their uplifting newsletter. This wonderful publication is full of real-life success stories , poems, recipes, talents and other actual submissions...all from people just like you and me. For your free issue send $1.00 for postage & handling & ask for sample issue of *"Positive Prospector"*. Mail to:

THE POSITIVE PROSPECTOR
PO BOX 195
HOLMER, WI 54636

MONEY SAVING TIPS

The publishers of *"Quick, Easy, Cheap and Simple"* newsletter would like to send a sample issue. It's loaded with information in the form of handy, easy-to-understand tips, on the all important topics of saving both time and money. You'll also find an assortment of quick and easy recipe ideas. For your free newsletter, mail a SASE to:

QUICK, EASY, CHEAP AND SIMPLE
4057 N. DRAKE-RP5
CHICAGO, IL 60618-2219

"SMART PLAY"

How do you shop for toys in this new age of modern technology? If you carefully select the correct electronic toy, you'll be able to find one that will both entertain and educate your child. To find the best educational toys for your kids, ask for *"Smart Play: A Guide to Learning & Discovering with Toys"*, send an SASE to:

VTECH SMART PLAY OFFER
380 W. PALATINE RD.
WHEELING, IL 60090

MEALTIMES

Would you like to receive an informative booklet and healthy feeding plan chart for your baby? You will also receive two 50¢ off coupons for Gerber products. Send a postcard to:

"MEALTIMES"
P.O. BOX 500
FREMONT, MI 49412

GARGOYLES

If you are a lover of Gargoyles, this catalog is for you. Gargoyles can be used as table bases, bird feeders, bookends, wall mountings, and sculptures indoor and outdoor. If you have some creative ideas for this stone-faced creatures, send a card to:

DESIGN TOSCANO OF CHICAGO
15 E. CAMPBELL ST., DEPT. 805
ARLINGTON HEIGHTS, IL 60005
OR CALL: 800-525-0733

SMART WIGS

For the best prices on the finest wigs send for your free catalog. You will be amazed at the beautiful selection of wigs from Revlon, Adolfo and many more. So if you are in the market for a wig write to:

BEAUTY TREND
PO BOX 9323, DEPT. 44002
HIALEAH, FL 33014.

NEWS FOR YOU

This freebie is for adults whose reading levels is grade 4 to 6, and is a great way to help improve their skills. Each issue contains articles covering important international news as well as features on education, health, leisure, law, etc. To get a free sample, ask for *News For You Sample Copy.* Write to:

NEW READERS PRESS
DEPT. 100, PO BOX 888
SYRACUSE, NY 13210

"BRIDAL TOASTING TIPS"

Martini & Rossi Asti Spumante share with you all the traditions of the bridal toast from around the world. Included in your freebie are suggested toasts for nervous members of the wedding party; also a wine serving guide and ideas for starting new traditions. Ask for *Bridal Toasting Tips.* Send a SASE to:

THE ALDEN GROUP
DEPT. M, 52 VANDERBILT AVE
NEW YORK, NY 10017

BEAD KIT

The Frantz Bead Company has put together an informative newsletter and supply catalog to teach you the art of bead making. You'll receive a free newsletter plus a catalog with a full range of terrific bead supplies. So if you're looking for an interesting and challenging hobby, send a postcard to:

FRANTZ BEAD COMPANY
1222 SUNSET HILL ROAD
SHELTON, WA 98584

CHOOSING TOYS

Properly selected toys can teach as well as amuse your child. Learn how to choose toys for children of all ages. The *toy information series* will allow you to enter and direct the young child's world. Yours free from:

TOY MANUFACTURERS OF AMERICA
200 FIFTH AVE.
NEW YORK, NY 10010

SHOP EASY

Relax and shop at home. Lillian Vernon's *free catalog is* full of affordable treasures from around the world. Drop a postcard to:

LILLIAN VERNON
VIRGINIA BEACH, VA 23479

CLASSIC GIFTS

Harriet Carter has provided distinctive gifts since 1958. This fun-filled catalog is chuck-full of unique gifts you will find fascinating. Write to:

HARRIET CARTER
DEPT. 14
NORTH WALES, PA 19455

GET THAT BUG

The makers of Raid bug sprays would like you to have a highly informative chart, *"Raid Insecticides - What to Use For Effective Control."* Learn how to deal with crawling, flying and biting pests both inside and outside your home (including plant pests). You'll also receive a money-saving coupon. Send a postcard to:

"INSECT CONTROL"
JOHNSON WAX
RACINE, WI 53403

COOPERATIVE EXTENSION

Your local cooperative extension office offers an amazing range of free information and services to all who request them. Soil analysis, 4-H information, home economics classes and money-management workshops are just a few of the services available. Call your local Extension Service. It's listed under "County Government" in the phone book.

ART FILMS

To help bring art appreciation to a wider audience The National Gallery of Art would like to send you a film without charge. They have dozens of films and slide programs to lend to individuals, community groups, schools, etc. Your only obligation is to pay the postage when sending the film back. For a complete *catalog and reservation card* send a card to:

NATIONAL GALLERY OF ART
EXTENSION PROGRAM
WASHINGTON, DC 20565

FREE TICKETS TO TV SHOWS

The TV networks will provide you with free tickets to any of their shows that have audiences. If you plan to be in Los Angeles or New York and would like to see a TV show write to the network (care of their 'Ticket Department') before your visit. Generally you will get a letter you can exchange for tickets for any show open at the time of your visit. Write to:

ABC, 415 PROSPECT AVE., LOS ANGELES, CA 90028

CBS TICKET DIV., TELEVISION CITY 7800 BEVERLY BLVD., LOS ANGELES, CA 90036

NBC, 3000 WEST ALAMEDA AVE.. BURBANK, CA 91523 (OR 30 ROCKEFELLER PLAZA, NEW YORK, NY 10020)

"EXCEPTIONAL BLACK SCIENTISTS" POSTERS

Blacks have made significant contributions in the field of science. To honor some of the more exceptional black scientists CIBA GEIGY has

prepared a beautiful set of *color posters* suitable for framing. If you'd like a free set write to:
CONSUMER RELATIONS
CIBA GEIGY CORP.
ARDSLEY, **NY 10502**

FOR THE LARGER-SIZED OR TALLER WOMAN

Lane Bryant offers a stunning collection of dresses, coats, jeans, sportswear, lingerie and shoes to the woman who wears half size or large size apparel. You'll find name brands and designer fashions in their free *catalog.* If you are 5'7" or taller also ask for their *Tall Collection catalog.* Write:
LANE BRYANT
DEPT. A
INDIANAPOLIS, **IN 46201**

CONSUMER COMPLAINTS

If you ever wanted to complain to a company about one of their products but didn't know how to go about it, this is for you. *"How To Talk To A Company And Get Action"* should help you get your problem solved—fast. You'll also receive the "Story of Coca Cola". Write to:
CONSUMER INFORMATION CENTER
COCA-COLA CO.
DEPT. FR, P.O. DRAWER 1734
ATLANTA, **GA 30301**

MILK SENSITIVE?

If you are allergic to milk you will want to get a copy of 'Ross's Educational Materials Catalog' designed specifically for those with a lactose intolerance. Write to:
EDUCATIONAL SERVICES
ROSS LABORATORIES
COLUMBUS, **OH 43216**

DENTURE ADHESIVE SAMPLE

For over 50 years Klutch has been a denture adhesive powder you can count on. Find out why denture wearers from coast to coast have confidence in Klutch. To receive a free sample plus a discount coupon, drop a card for a *free sample* to:

KLUTCH HANDY TRIAL SIZE
I. PUTNAM INC.
BOX 444
BIG FLATS, NY 14814

BOYS CLUB

Give your boys things to do and a place to go to develop their character. The Boys Clubs of America have been doing this for over 100 years. They have 1100 local chapters in 700 towns. Ask for the *"Boy's Club Information Package."* Write to:
BOYS CLUB OF AMERICA
771 FIRST AVE.
NEW YORK, NY 10017

FINDING THE RIGHT CAMP OR SCHOOL

Choosing the right sleepaway camp or private school can be very confusing. To help take the confusion out of camp or school shopping here's a helpful booklet, *"How To Choose A Camp For Your Child."* Send a SASE to:
AMERICAN CAMPING ASSN.
5000 STATE RD.
67 NORTH
MARTINSVILLE, IN 46151

YOUR OWN FLAG OVER THE CAPITOL

Your Congressman will provide a unique service for you free of charge. If you'd like to have your own flag flown over the U.S. Capitol Building write to your congressman. The flag itself is not free (prices range from $8.00 to $17.00 depending upon size and material) but the service of having the flag purchased, flown and sent to you is free. This also makes a unique gift for someone special. Write to your own Congressman,
CONGRESS OF THE UNITED STATES
WASHINGTON, DC 20515

PRESERVE OUR HISTORY

If you'd like to participate in the preservation

of sites, buildings and objects that are important to American history and culture, there is something you can do. Drop a card asking for the *Historic Preservation package* to:

NATIONAL TRUST FOR HISTORIC PRESERVATION
1785 MASSACHUSETTS AVE. N.W.
WASHINGTON, DC 20036

CONSUMER HANDBOOK

A problem everyone has at one time or another is who to turn to when he has a complaint. Now with the *Consumer Resource Handbook* you will know the best non-government and government sources to contact for help. This is something no one should be without. Send a card to:

CONSUMER RESOURCE HANDBOOK
CONSUMER INFORMATION CENTER
PUEBLO, CO 91009

YOUR OWN MONEYTREE

Wouldn't it be great to have your very own moneytree growing in a corner of your kitchen? American companies give away billions of dollars of gifts, cash, sweepstakes and freebies every year. The editors of MoneyTree Digest show you how to get your share of the Great American Giveaway. To get a sample issue of this terrific magazine, send $1.00 postage & handling to:

MONEYTREE DIGEST
648 CENTRAL AVE. SUITE 441-BFT
SCARSDALE, NY 10583

POPCORN PANDEMONIUM

Love popcorn? Ready for something different? Why not try rum butter toffee, peanut butter, fruit salad or cinnamon flavored popcorn? The Popcorn Factory has everything you ever dreamed of in popcorn, jelly beans, pretzels, nuts and home poppers. For a free catalog, write to:

THE POPCORN FACTORY
MAIL ORDER DEPT.
PO BOX 453
LAKE BLUFF, IL 60044

BUYING LIFE INSURANCE

Buying the right amount and the right type of life insurance is one of the important decisions

you must make. Before you make any decision, be sure to get your copy of *"How To Choose A Life Insurance Company"*. To get your copy of this informative booklet, simply send a postcard to:
OCCIDENTAL LIFE
BOX 2101 TERMINAL ANNEX
LOS ANGELES, CA 90051

CHAPPED LIPS?

If you suffer from dry chapped lips or mouth sores, this is especially for you. You will receive sample packets of Blistex Lip Ointment plus two informative brochures and a 25¢-off coupon too. Send a long SASE to:
BLISTEX SAMPLE OFFER
1800 SWIFT DR.
OAK BROOK, IL 60521

LOVE FRAGRANCES

If you love all those expensive perfumes and colognes advertised on TV, radio and magazines but don't want to pay the high prices, this is a must for you. For your free list and scented cards, drop a card to:
ESSENTIAL PRODUCTS CO. INC.
90 WATER ST.
NEW YORK, NY 10005

THE COMPANY STORE

If you are looking for a superior blend of hand selected white goose and duck down feather comforters, pillows or outerwear this is the place for you. Drop a card for their *free catalog* to:
THE COMPANY STORE
500 COMPANY STORE ROAD
LA GROSSE, WI 54601

WORDS OF WISDOM

If you need words of encouragement to keep going in the face of adversity (and who doesn't), "Portrait of An Achiever" is an inspirational addition to any home. This beautiful parchment reproduction is suitable for framing and makes an excellent gift. Send $1.00 s&h to:
ROBLIN PRESS

405 Tarrytown Rd Suite 414 - POA
White Plains, NY 10607

MAIL ORDER BUYING

Here is a practical and informative guide detailing the protection you have under the F.T.C.'s Mail Order Merchandise Rule. A free copy of *"Shopping By Phone & Mail"* is yours by writing to:

Shopping by Phone and Mail
Department P
Federal Trade Commission
Washington, DC 20580

"SCHOOL ZONE"

If you are a parent, you want to help build a solid foundation of important basic skills for your child. This *free catalog* will help you encourage learning and prepare your child for the future. Write:

School Zone Publishing
PO Box 777
Grand Haven, MI 49417

SHIPS AND THE SEA

This 100 page *catalog is* full of decorative nautical ideas for the home. If you're looking for a ship model, marine painting or ship's wheel you'll find it here. Drop a postcard to:

Preston's
174-A Main St. Wharf
Greenport, NY 11944

FLAGS

If you are looking for any kind of flags, poles and accessories, custom designs states, nations, historic and nautical, this *free catalog* has them all. Write to:

Chris Reid
P.O. Box 1827SM
Midlothian, VA 23113

FREE FROM THE PRESIDENT

Imagine the excitement of getting a letter from the President. The President will send a signed card embossed with the Presidential seal to any couple celebrating their 50th anniversary (or beyond) or to any citizen celebrating their 80th (or subsequent) birthday. At the other end of the spectrum, the President will also send a congratulatory card to any newborn child. What a great gift!! Send your requests at least 4 weeks in advance to:

THE GREETINGS OFFICE
THE WHITE HOUSE
WASHINGTON, DC 20500

FREE FROM THE WHITE HOUSE

The President would like you to have a beautiful full color book, "The White House, The House of The People." It features a room-by-room photo tour and history of the White House. For your free copy write to:

THE WHITE HOUSE
WASHINGTON, DC 20500

A MOVING EXPERIENCE

To help you with your next move United Van Lines has set up a toll free number you can call. Their Consumer Service Center is set up to answer any specific questions you may have. For example, they can answer your questions about employment, educational facilities, housing, and more, in 7,000 cities and towns throughout the 50 states (and foreign countries too). They can also provide you with numerous guides and booklets which make preplanning a lot easier. Call: **1-800-325-3870**, (in Missouri call collect: 314-326-3100), or send a SASE to:

CONSUMER SERVICES CENTER
UNITED VAN LINES
ONE UNITED DR.
FENTON, MO 63026

PLANNING A MOVE

Mayflower has a nice packet of moving materials free for the asking. It includes labels to mark your boxes with plus tips to make your move run smoother and faster. Ask for your *"Moving Kit"* from your local Mayflower mover or send a

card to:
MAYFLOWER MOVERS
BOX 107B
INDIANAPOLIS, IN 46206

PEACE CORPS

The Peace Corps can give you the chance to immerse yourself in a totally different culture while helping to make an important difference in other people's lives. If you like helping people and want to get involved, get the *Peace Corps Information package.* Call toll-free: **1-800-424-8580**

DECIDED TO MOVE?

How To Stretch Your Moving Budget – The Interstate Moving Guide is a useful pamphlet that will help you make your interstate move run smoothly. It tells you how to prepare for moving day, how moving costs are calculated, a glossary of moving terms and lots more. It's your free from:
ATLAS VAN LINES
1212 ST. GEORGE RD.
EVANSVILLE, IN 47703.

KEEP WARM

Stay warm this winter with insulated clothing, outdoor equipment and toasty down comforters that you make yourself — with the help of a Frostline kit. For a copy of their free catalog, send a postcard to:
FROSTLINE KITS
2525 RIVER ROAD.
GRAND JUNCTION, CO 81505

FASHION EASE

Fashion Ease specializes in clothing for elderly, arthritic or handicapped people. Styles wrap and close easily with Velcro or snaps. There are wheelchair accessories and items for the incontinent. To get a copy of their free catalog write to:
FASHION EASE
541 60TH ST.
BROOKLYN, NY 11219

PET ALLERGIES

If you are allergic to pets there may be a new way to eliminate those allegies around the house with a new vacuum by Nilfisk, Inc. of America. Call:
1-800-241-9420 EXT 2

HERE ARE A FEW TOLL-FREE HOTLINES YOU CAN CALL FOR SPECIAL UP-TO-THE MINUTE INFORMATION ON IMPORTANT TOPICS

CONSUMER HELPLINES

For general consumer problems, questions and complaints and where and how to get action, call the Consumer Helpline:
1-800-664-4435 BETWEEN **10** A.M. AND **2** P.M.

HEADACHE HOTLINE

The American Council for Headache Education may offer a solution on how to lessen your pain and discomfort
1-800-255-ACHE

ASTHMA INFORMATION

If you suffer from asthma, you will want to get a free copy of *"Making The Most of Your Next Doctor Visit."* You will discover what you can do to assist your doctor in helping you relieve your asthma suffering. Call:
1-800-456-2784

CARPET CARE

If you are thinking of adding or changing carpets in your home but are confused by the many choices you have to make, call The Carpet and Rug Institute information line for answers to your questions related to carpeting your home
1-800-882-8846

HAIR REMOVAL

Nudit allows women to discuss with experts the sensitive issue of hair removal treatments. Their hotline number is:
1-800-62-NUDIT

Music

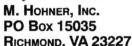

HOHNER HARMONICAS

Hohner, probably the best known name in harmonicas (including one that's 2 feet long) would like you to have a copy of *"How to Play the Hohner Harmonica."* It is a step-by-step concise guide and song book. It also shows how to get special effects from your harmonica. For your free copy write:

M. Hohner, Inc.
PO Box 15035
Richmond, VA 23227

INTEREST YOUR CHILD IN MUSIC

Getting a youngster interested in playing a musical instrument can be quite a chore for a parent. *"How Music Can Bring You Closer To Your Child"* may make that task a little easier. Yours free from:

G. Leblanc Corp.
7019 30th Ave.
Kenosha, WI 53141

PANASONIC CATALOG

For a *color catalog* of all Panasonic products including radio's, TV's, CB's, tape recorders and VCRs— write to:

Panasonic
One Panasonic Way
Secaucus, NJ 07094

HUGE MUSIC & ELECTRONICS CATALOG

J & R Music World's catalog with over 10,000 products is actually one of the most comprehensive product source books in the audio, video, computer and electronics field. It features all major brand names—everything in home entertainment. For a free copy of this 304 page catalog, call toll-free: (800) 221-8180 or send a postcard to:

J & R Music World
23 Park Row
New York,, NY 10038
(In NYC call 212-732-8600)

Craft & Hobbies

FASCINATING FOLDS

Bet you never knew just how much fun folding paper can be! Learn the fascinating craft of Origami- Japanese paper folding and turn simple paper into a work of art. Great teaching tool for math. Learn to make flying birds, flowers, animals and much more! Send $1 postage & handling to:

FASCINATING FOLDS
PO BOX 2820-235
TORRANCE CA 90509-2820

"HOT SHOTS WITH ANY CAMERA"

This 48 page guide in full color shows you how to take the best snapshots under any circumstances. It's easy to understand and deals with topics such as lighting, flash photography, action and more. So start taking better pictures now. Ask for *"Hot Shots With Any Camera."* Call:
1-800-242-2424

PLAYING BETTER CHESS

Learn the official rules of this challenging game of chess and also receive another publication to join the U.S. Chess Federation. Chess helps you develop your ability to think analytically. Ask for *"Ten Tips To Winning Chess."* Send a SASE to:

U.S. CHESS FEDERATION
DEPT. 17, 186 ROUTE 9W
NEW WINDSOR, NY 12553
OR CALL: **1-800-388-KING**

BLACK JACK"

A free Black Jack Strategy Card is yours for the asking. This pocket-sized card gives you invaluable strategies, based on what you are dealt and what the tester is showing. Various combinations of hands and dealer show cards are printed right on an easy to read chart. Gambling ...blackjack in particular...can be fun if you're able to combine luck with a little strategy. Ask

for *Black Jack Strategy Card* write to:
THOMAS GAMING SERVICES
PO BOX 1383
GOLETA, CA 93116

CROCHET TIME

These free crochet instructions will show you how to make some beautiful hand made ornaments, that you could sell, give as gifts or enjoy yourself. You can make seven simple thread snowflakes and 10 easy yarn ornaments. So get started now and send for your free instructions. Ask for: Crochet Tree-Trim Pattern, SASE to:

LORRAINE VETTER-FT
7924 SOPER HILL ROAD
EVERETT, WA 98205

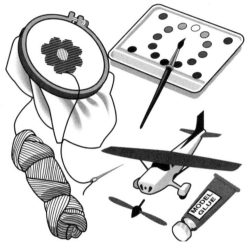

FREE PATTERN

Crocheting Forever has a great freebie for you. They'll send you a free fashion doll wedding gown pattern. It comes with detailed instructions and illustrations and will teach your child the art of crocheting. This beautiful finished ruffled dress fits all dolls even Mattel's Barbie. Ask for *Doll Dress Crochet Pattern*. Send a SASE to:
CROCHETING FOREVER
20021 FOX STREET
Cassopolis, MI 49031

HOME SEWING BASICS

If you're thinking of decorating anything from a single room to an entire house, be sure to get *"Sewing - It's Sew Soothing.* Discover how much fun it is to make your own curtains, slip covers and pillow shams. To get your copy, send a long SASE to:

AMERICAN HOME SEWING AND CRAFT ASSOCIATION
1375 BROADVIEW
NEW YORK, NY 10018

BEAT THE ODDS

Thousands of people love the challenge and excitement of blackjack. If this describes you, you may have wondered if there was any way you could improve your chances of winning. To help you better your odds, send for a wallet-size free mini-magnetic strategy card. Send a SASE and ask for "Winning Blackjack Strategies" to:

S. J. LEE ENTERPRISES
PO BOX 333-H, DEPT. BFT
SCARSDALE, NY 10583

POLAROID PROBLEMS?

Have your Polaroid photos been coming out the way you'd like? There's a toll-free hotline to call where an expert will answer any questions you may have. Call toll free 8AM -8PM Mon- Sat. at **800-343-5000.** Polaroid has a commendable policy of complete customer satisfaction. Your problem may lie with defective film which they'll replace at no charge. Send defective film or photos to:

POLAROID CUSTOMER CARE SERVICE
784 MEMORIAL DR.
CAMBRIDGE, MA 02139

PICTURE THIS

Kodak has several excellent guides to help improve your photo-taking skills. *"Picture-Taking-A Self Teaching Guide"* is a do-it yourself mini-course that will help you take better pictures. Free from:

EASTMAN KODAK CO.
343 STATE ST.
ROCHESTER, NY 14650

PLAYING DUPLICATE BRIDGE

If you're a Bridge player, you'll want this catalog and product source guide. Write to:

AMERICAN CONTRACT BRIDGE LEAGUE

2990 AIRWAYS BLVD.
P.O. BOX 161192
MEMPHIS, TN 38116

"HAVE A HOBBY"

If you'd like to develop a new and interesting hobby consider paper crafts (origami, paper sculpture, quilling or paper snipping) or decoupage — decorating with paper cutouts. Send a long SASE, to:
HOBBY INDUSTRY OF AMERICA
319 E. 54TH ST.
ELMWOOD PARK, NJ 07407

"HOW TO MAKE PLAY CLAY"

Create your own gifts, decorations and jewelry with play clay. You'll learn how to make play clay from Arm & Hammer Baking Soda. Ask for *"Play Clay"* & drop a card to:
ARM & HAMMER CONSUMER RELATIONS
DIVISION OF CHURCH & DWIGHT CO.
PRINCETON, NJ 08543-5297 OR CALL:
1-800-524-1328

BEAUTIFUL LETTERS

If you are interested in learning how to create handcrafted lettering, this is for you. With the *Hunt Lettering Charts* you will receive a super collection of Roman Gothic, Old English and Manuscript lettering charts plus helpful hints. Send a card to:
HUNT BIENFANG PAPER CO.
2020 W. FRONT ST.
STATESVILLE, NC

PICTURE PERFECT

Kodak has a freebie for all of you who want to take those perfect pictures. Give them a call and ask for *"365 Days to Better Pictures"* call:
(1-800-599-5929)

THE ART OF VENTRILOQUISM

Here is your chance to learn about what a ventriloquist is and how to become one. You will also learn how to build a puppet and even put together and market a show. You will learn how to start, the direction to go in and more. Remember Howdy Doody, and Edgar and Jerry Mahoney? Well you can learn all the same techniques they used. To receive this 32 page booklet on how to become a ventriloquist write to :

THE NORTH AMERICAN ASSOCIATION OF
VENTRILOQUISTS
BOX 420
LITTLETON CO 80160

MECHANICAL TOYS

If you are a collector of fine mechanical toys, this beautifully illustrated catalog is for you. In the 32 pages of this catalog you will find a unique collection of classic cars. Ask for Lilliput Catalog from:

LILLIPUT
PO BOX 447
YERINGTON, NV 89447
OR CALL: 1-800-TIN-TOTS

ZIPPO COLLECTORS

Somewhere in your attic or basement you my stumble across an old Zippo lighter, know for their reliability and quality for over 50 years. To find out whether your old Zippo has any real value today, ask for a *Collectors Guide* :

ZIPPO MANUFACTURING CO.
33 BARBOUN ST.
BRADFORD, PA

OLD-TIME STAMPS

There's an old-time collection of 26 different stamps waiting for you. Each stamp is 50 to 100 years old. The stamps are worth $2.00 at catalog prices but are yours for only 50 cents postage. You'll also receive other stamps on approval but there's no obligation to buy anything. Write to:

FALCON STAMP CO.
072 ST
FALCONER, NY 14733

START A STAMP CLUB

If you're interested in collecting stamps you might enjoy the company of other stamp collectors. For a free copy of *"You Can Start A Stamp Club"*. Write to:

AMERICAN PHILATELIC SOCIETY
P.O. Box 8000
STATE COLLEGE, PA 16801.

NUMISMATIC NEWS

Here's a newspaper coin collectors will want to have. Simply write and request a free copy of *'Numismatic Weekly.'* You'll enjoy its many interesting articles. Send a card to:

NUMISMATIC NEWS WEEKLY
IOLA, WI 54990

COMIC BOOK COLLECTORS

If you enjoy collecting old comic books, you will want to send for a giant list of back issues of Marvel comics. Send 35¢ postage to:

R. Crestohl
4732 Circle Rd.
Montreal, Canada.

For Pet Lovers

NEW PUPPY/NEW KITTEN

If you're thinking of getting a new puppy or kitten this freebie from Iams Company is for you. *"You & Your New Puppy? You & Your New Kitten"* gives you useful advice on feeding, housetraining, health care, grooming, training of a new pet-and more. Write to:

THE IAMS COMPANY
PUPPY/KITTEN INFORMATION CENTER
BOX 1475
DAYTON, OHIO 45401

"CARING FOR YOUR DOG"

If you have a dog or are planning to get one, make sure you write for the book "Caring For Your Dog." The folks at Ralston Purina dog food products have prepared this excellent book that will not only give you a brief history of dogs, but also give you tips on feeding your dog, grooming, obedience training, keeping your dog healthy and traveling with your dog. They will include discount coupons and a *Purina Dog Food Guide* to balancing nutrients to meet your dog's needs. Also ask for *"Guide To Health Care For Your Dog."* This freebie is a must if you ever thought of getting a dog for a pet. Write to:

RALSTON PURINA
DOG FOOD DIVISION
CHECKERBOARD SQUARE
ST. LOUIS, MO 63164.

FOR THE BIRDS

Lafeber's Avi-Cakes Gourmet Bird Food will provide a perfectly nutritious snack to satisfy bird munchies. Avi-Cakes is a nutritionally complete bird treat with proper vitamins and delicious flavors. Get your free trial size sample now. Ask for: *Avi-Cakes Sample* Write to:

LAFEBER COMPANY
RR #2
ODELL, IL 60460

FISH ARE FUN

Fish are educational, fun and something the whole family can enjoy. Now you can learn step-by-step how to set up a year round backyard pond and stock it with hardy fish. Send for your free *"We Are The Water Garden Experts"* Drop a postcard to:
TETRA POND
3001 COMMERCE ST.
BLACKSBURG, VA 24060-6671

GAINES FOODS

Gaines foods has a number of informative publications that are yours for the asking. Write for the free publications list to:
QUAKER PROFESSIONAL SERVICES
585 HAWTHORNE COURT #14
GALESBURG, IL 61401

MORE THAN A FRIEND

To millions of people their pet is a real member of the family. And love of animals has inspired many to follow a career path to becoming a veterinarian. For these people the American Veterinary Association has an interesting booklet called *"Today's Veterinarian"* about the opportunities available today in this interesting field. For your free copy send a postcard to:
AMERICAN VETERINARY ASSOCIATION
1931 NORTH MEECHAM RD. SUITE 100,
SCHAUMBURG, IL 60196

CARE FOR YOUR PETS

The American Humane Association has a whole series of informative booklets available for pet owners. These booklets tell how to care for dogs, cats, horses, birds and fish. For a complete listing, write for their free *catalog of publications.* From:
AMERICAN HUMANE ASSOCIATION
P.O. BOX 1266
DENVER, CO 80201

PET CARE & NUTRITION

If you'd like any information about proper pet care and pet nutrition, the makers of Kal Kan pet food would like to help you. They will send you *"Understanding Your Dog" and "Understanding Your Cat."* Write to:

KAL KAN CONSUMER ADVISORY SERVICE
3386 EAST 44TH ST.
P.O. BOX 58853
VERNON, CA 90058

Cookbooks

The companies giving away these free cookbooks and recipe collections do so at great expense as their way of saying "thank you" to their loyal customers. They also hope to inspire you to even greater use of their products by showing you new and innovative ways of using them to create meals you and your family will enjoy. It is always a nice idea to mention, however briefly, how much you enjoy using their products.

A-1 STEAK SAUCE RECIPE
Learn all the great tasting meals you can make by using A-1 Steak sauce in new and innovative ways. Ask for *A-1 Steak Sauce Recipe Book* from:
NABISCO FOODS, INC.
PO BOX 1928
EAST HANOVER, NJ 07936-1928

MEAT & POULTRY HOTLINE
The USDA has a meat and poultry hotline to help you with questions dealing with food safety. There are a full series of recorded answers to the most commonly asked question or if you have specific questions, you can speak with a food safety expert. Call weekdays from 10:00am–4:00pm (Eastern Time) to speak to a specialist. For recorded messages, you can call 24 hours a day.
1-800 535-4555

A GREAT TIME TO BE FRENCH
If you would like a free reference guide to French wine, cheeses and ham, call:
1-800-522-WINE

CHANGING COURSES
For great recipes using reduced fat sour cream ask for *Changing Courses* recipe collection. Call:
1-800-782-9602

KERR KITCHEN PANTRY

The Kerr Kitchen Pantry has a wonderful newsletter that they will send to you just for the asking. This informative newsletter will give you all kinds of great tips for canning, freezing fresh vegetables and fruits. There are great recipes of the season as well as some helpful hints for homemakers. You'll also find some great canning recipes for relish, sauces and jelly. Ask for the "Kerr Kitchen Pantry." Write to:

CONSUMER PRODUCTS DIVISION
KERR GROUP
1840 CENTURY PARK EAST
LOS ANGELES, CA 90067

NOODLE-LINE

Are you always in a hurry to prepare a new nutritious main dish. Call the Rice-A-Roni/ Noodle-Roni Main Dish Helpline. Call this computerized phone service will help you put together a great meals in less than 30 minutes. You will also receive quick to prepare rice and pasta recipes. Call **1-800-421-2444** Or write to:

GOLDEN GRAIN CO.
PO BOX 651230
SALT LAKE CITY, UT 84165

HOT POTATO

Are you constantly wondering what you can do to make dinner more interesting? Learn why potatoes are America's favorite vegetable and new ways to prepare and serve this healthy vegetable. Ask for *"Dinnertime Dilemma. Answers to That Age-Old Question."* Send a long SASE to:

"DINNERTIME DILEMMA,"
DEPT PA, 55 UNION STREET
SAN FRANCISCO, CA 94111

COOKIE LOVERS

The ultimate cookie is here. Saco Foods will send you these ten delicious recipes plus a 20 cents off coupon. Create a chocolate sensation today with these delicious chocolate chunks.

Remember it's the chocolate that counts. Now it's easy to get more sweet satisfaction in each bite! They even have a *Bake Your Best Hot line* **(800-373-SACO).** Or send a SASE to:
SACO FOODS
FREE COOKIE OFFER
PO BOX 616
MIDDLETOWN, WI 53562

FREE CALORIE GUIDE

Thanks to the people at Weight Watchers with this handy calorie guide you'll be able to count calories even when you dine out. It's 32 pages full of calorie counts for the most popular restaurant and fast food style dishes. Ask for: *Dining Out Calorie Guide*. Mail a SASE to:
WEIGHT WATCHERS MAGAZINE DINING OUT GUIDE
360 LEXINGTON AVE.
NEW YORK, NY 10017

DELI-DELICIOUS

"Easy Entertaining-Award -Winning Deli Meat Recipes" contains 12 recipes for perfect party platters. Preparation times and even calorie counts accompany the recipes. This wonderful freebie comes to you from the National Live Stock and Meat Board. Ask for *Easy Entertaining Brochure*. Just mail a SASE to:
NATIONAL LIVE STOCK AND MEAT BOARD
444 N. MICHIGAN AVE., DEPT. EE
CHICAGO, IL 60611

WHEN IN ROME

History shows that the Romans used clay cookware centuries ago. Clay retains moisture which is released slowly during cooking resulting in savory self-basted food. For a terrific collection of recipes using clay Brique Ware, ask for *"Brique Ware Recipes" and "Microwaving with Nordic Ware."* Free from:
CUSTOMER SERVICE NORDIC WARE
HIGHWAY 7 AT 100
MINNEAPOLIS, MN 55416

HOT STUFF

Red Devil Hot Sauce is a zesty hot sauce that has dozens of uses—in soups, stews, sandwiches and just about anywhere you want to add a lively taste to your food. For a compact collection of dozens of recipes, send a card asking for *"Seasoning With Trappey's Red Devil Hot Sauce"* to:
B. F. TRAPPEY'S SONS
DRAWER 400
NEW IBERIA, LA 70560

SNAP, CRACKLE &...NUTRITION

When is a Rice Krispie more than a Rice Krispie? When it's part of a well-balanced nutrition program. The people at Kellogg's would like to show you how to serve your family more nutritious meals. Send for *"Kellogg's Favorite Recipes"* free from:
DEPARTMENT OF HOME ECONOMICS
KELLOGG CO.
BATTLE CREEK, MI 49016

FISH REALLY IS GOOD FOR YOU

Research has proven that eating fish is really good for you. According to the National Fisheries Institute, the average person eats a total of about 15 pounds of fish per year, or 4 1/2 ounces per week. Among the top 10 choices are salmon (fourth) and catfish (sixth). The Catfish Institute has three recipe brochures waiting for you. In them you'll find a variety of ideas besides traditional high-fat frying. They can be ordered free by calling:
1-888-451-FISH

COOKING LIGHT

We all know that what we eat affects our health. But exactly what foods are the best for our health? How do you prepare foods that are good for you? Now there's a toll-free number you can call for answers to these and other questions you may have. This hotline sponsored by the

Healthy Cooking magazine will put you in touch with registered dietitians who will answer your questions about cooking light. Call between 9 a.m. and 5:30 p.m. weekdays
1-800-231-3438

BAKERS HOTLINE
Fleishmann's Yeast Bakers Help Line, specializes answering your questions about yeast and bread-baking, including advice on using bread machines. Call weekdays between 10 am and 8pm.
(1-800) 777-4959

"GOLDEN BLOSSOM"
Many say that Golden Blossom Honey is the tastiest honey there is. To show you how to use their sweet necter in new ways they will send you a nice collection of recipes. Just call and ask for the free Golden Blosssom recipes collection. Call:
1-800-220-2110

GRILL-OUT
If you love to barbacue, call The Weber Grill Hotline at **1-800-GRILL-OUT** and get answers to all your barbecue questions including cooking methods, fat trimming tips and clean up to recipes, steak cooking hints and food safety tips. You'll also receive a free guide with loads of great barbecue recipes. Ask for *More Backyard Barbecue Basics*. Or write to:
WEBER
BOX BAH
200 EAST DANIELS RD.
PALATINE, IL 60067

FOOD FASTS
The Department of Agriculture has a large package of fascinating and educational materials including a handy food pyramid guide waiting for you. Learn exactly what the USDA does in the areas of consumer services, food safety, nutrition and lots more. Excellent teaching and learning tool. Write to:

U.S. DEPARTMENT OF AGRICULTURE
PUBLICATIONS DIV.
WASHINGTON, DC 20250.
OR YOU CAN ACCESS THEIR HOME PAGE ON THE
WORLDWIDE WEB AT INTERNET ADDRESS: http://
www.usda.gov

EATING HEALTHY

AARP has a nutrition guide with information on dietary guidelines, the food pyramid, the new food labels and special diets for a better quality of life. To get a free copy of *"Healthy Eating For a Healthy Life"* (stock #D15565), send a postcard to:
AARP FULFILLMEMNT EE0924
601 E STREET N.W.
WASHINGTON, D.C. 20049

CHEESE RECIPES

Six cheese recipes on file cards are available free from Marin French Cheese Company. Also included will be a mail order price list for their fine line of cheeses. Free from:
MARIN FRENCH CHEESE CO.
7500 RED HILL RD.
PETALUMA, CA 94953

POPPIN' FRESH DOUGH

Pillsbury brings you some prize winning recipes...cakes from scratch, easy yeast baking...all kinds of refrigerated dough ideas. All this to help make your next dessert a sweet and tasty delight. Yours free from:
PILLSBURY CO.
CONSUMER RESPONSE
P.O. BOX 550
MINNEAPOLIS, MN 55440

DE-LIGHT TORTILLAS

To help you add a 'south of the border' touch to your next meal, the folks at Mission Foods would like to send you *"The Art of Light Tortillas"*. Learn how to make a delightful Spanish

Pizza, Strawberry Breakfast Crepes, Fiesta Crab Crisps and lots more.
CALL TOLL FREE: **1-800-600-TACO**

POPCORN LOVERS

If popcorn is a favorite of yours *"Favorite Popcorn Recipes"* is a must. It features mouth-watering popcorn balls, zesty treats and sweet 'n munchy snacks. Drop a postcard to:
AMERICAN POPCORN CO.
BOX 178
SIOUX CITY, IA 51102

SWEET TOOTH

Looking for new dessert ideas your whole family will enjoy? You'll find lots of yummy dessert recipes and also learn how to cut the fat from sweets with *Plum Good* recipe. For your free copy and discount coupon, write to:
SOKOL & CO.
5315 DANSHER RD.
COUNTRYSIDE, IL 60525

PASTA - A FOOD FOR TODAY

Here are three excellent booklets for the health conscious. There are great recipes and lots of things you can add to pasta. There are even quick microwave dishes you can make. Ask for *Hershey Pasta Recipes* from:
HERSHEY PASTA GROUP
CONSUMER RELATIONS
PO BOX 815
HERSHEY, PA 17033

BREAKFAST & MORE

Roman Meal Company makes an excellent line of whole grain breads. The *Roman recipe collection* will show you how to make meals your family will love—like Porcupine Meatballs or Sloppy Joe's. You'll also receive budget stretcher ideas and low-fat diet menus. Free from:
ROMAN MEAL CO.

PO Box 11126
TACOMA, WA 98411

APPLE SAUCE
This great cookbook has some of the most delightful recipes using Lucky Leaf Apple Sauce. You will find recipes for everything from entrees to desserts. Yours free from:
KNOUSE FOODS
PEACH GLEN, PA 17306

SAUSAGE RECIPES
Discover many tasty new ways of enjoying sausages with the *Hillshire Farm Sausage recipes.* For your free copy send a postcard to:
HILLSHIRE FARMS
ROUTE 4, BOX 227
NEW LONDON, WI 54961

DINNER PANCAKES
From the makers of Mrs Butterworth's buttered syrup, comes a nice collection of budget recipes that will appeal to any palate. Send a postcard asking for *"Mrs. Butterworth's Inflation Fighting Recipes"* to:
LEVER BROTHERS CO.
390 PARK AVE.
NEW YORK, NY 10022

NOT FOR DIETERS
Here's a yummy collection of *"Hershey's Favorite Recipes."* Selections like Chocolate Peppermint Whirlaway Pie will make your mouth water just thinking about it. Your diet can wait 'til next month. Also ask for *"A Profile Of Hershey Foods."* Drop a card to:
CONSUMER INFORMATION
HERSHEY FOODS
HERSHEY, PA 17033
OR CALL: 1-800-468-1714

V.I.P. FROM IDAHO

"Heart Healthy" recipes will provide you with some tasty recipe plus handy tips on buying and storing Idaho Potatoes. Write to:

IDAHO POTATO COMMISSION
P.O. BOX 1068
BOISE, ID 83701

GEORGIA PEACH

Like peaches? You're gonna love Georgia Peach Cobler, Peach Salsa, and other low fat recipes using peaches. Send a long SASE and ask for *"Enjoy Georgia Peaches: A Southern Tradition"* to:

GEORGIA PEACH COMMISSION
BOX 38146
ATLANTA, GA 30334

DELICIOSA

If you are afraid to enjoy pasta meals just because you're on a diet— this one's for you. With *"Super Solutions For Super Suppers"* you will enjoy delicious Italian meals that are nutritionally balanced and still allow you to lose weight. You'll also receive a discount coupon. Send to:

RAGU FOODS, INC.
33 BENEDICT PL.
GREENWICH. CT 06830

"EXCELLENCE MADE EASY"

Grey Poupon Dijon Mustard has a sixteen page recipe book that features over 35 different ways to spice up your menu with Grey Poupon Dijon Mustard. Here are tasty recipe ideas for red meat, chicken, pasta, fish and more. Ask for *"Excellence Made Easy"* write:

NABISCO FOODS GROUP
GREY POUPON
PO BOX 720
HUDSON, WI 54016

SWEET AS AN...ONION?

An onion is probably the last thing you think

of when you think of sweet foods. Vidalia Onion would like to change your mind. These special onions are mild and tasty. They're grown
only in a small section of Georgia where
weather and soil conditions blend to make the
World's Sweetest Onion. Send today for the
Vidalia Onion recipe collection which will also
show you how to freeze and store these unique
onions. Send a SASE to:
VIDALIA ONION COMMITTEE
P.O. BOX 1609
VIDALIA, GA 30474

SEAFOOD DELIGHT

This compact collection of seafood recipe ideas
comes to you from Lassco Smoked Salmon.
You'll find tasty delights that'll make your next
barbecue more fun, and gourmet delicacies to
liven up any meal. Request "Seafood Recipes
from Lassco." Free from:
LASSCO
778 KOHLER ST.
LOS ANGELES, CA 90021

"MAINE SARDINE STORY"

Learn why fish is an excellent food for kids. Send
for a free copy of "Why Fish For Kids." Plus, for
the youngsters there's a fun comic book called
Ricky & Debbie in SardineLand that will entertain while it informs young people about the
great benefits of eating fish. All are free from:
MAINE SARDINE COUNCIL
470 N. MAIN ST.
BREWER, ME 04412

BASKET OF FRESH IDEAS

This collection of strawberry recipes
will show you how to use this
tasty fruit to make mouth
watering desserts and
drinks. Send a card to:
CALIFORNIA STRAWBERRY
ADVISORY BOARD
P.O. BOX 269
WATSONVILLE, CA 95077

"SIMPLY SWEET" RECIPES

NutraSweet Company has a nice package of easy to prepare recipes. Some of the things you will receive include, "Home Sweet Home With Equal - NutraSweet Spoonful Recipes, plus some simple tips for making food label information easy to understand and discount coupons. To get your free kit, write to:

E-Z SURVIVAL KIT
THE NUTRASWEET COMPANY
PO BOX 830
DEERFIELD, IL 60015
OR CALL THEIR TOLL-FREE NUMBER: **800-632-8935**

BEES & HONEY

Here's a double-barreled special. Fascinating facts about bees and honey plus a collection of taste tempting recipes using golden honey. Just ask for *"Cook It Right With Honey."* Send a card to:

DADANT & SONS
HAMILTON, IL 62341

TOP HITS FROM FRITO LAYS

This new recipe collection *""Baked Low Fat - Taste The Fun Not The Fat"* will provide you with a host of innovative new ways to enjoy Tostitos Tortilla Chips. Enjoy Chicken Curry Nachos or Italian Nachos. You'll also learn the story of Frito-Lay. Free from:

FRITO-LAY,
PO BOX 35034
DALLAS, TX 75235

BIRTHDAY PARTY PLANNER

Before you plan your child's next birthday party, be sure to send for this freebie. Skippy has put together some great party ideas from invitations to decorations and activities. Ask for *Skippy Peanut Butter Party Planner* from:

SKIPPY PEANUT BUTTER
DEPT. SPP, BOX 307
COVENTRY, CT 06238

A TOUCH OF TABASCO

Add a little zest to your next meal with these recipes using Tabasco sauce. Send a card asking for *"From The Land of Tabasco Sauce."* This cookbook features dozens of tangy and tasty meal ideas and recipes for everything from Holiday Turkey to Cream Onion Dip. Put a little spice in your life and your meals. Write to:
McILHENNY CO.
AVERY ISLAND, LA 70513

ADVENTURES IN GOOD EATING

Looking for new meal ideas your whole family will enjoy? Meals such as Stuffed Pork Chops and Tangy Chicken are among those you'll find in the *Heinz Recipe Collection.* Also ask for the *"Heinz Cooking With Beans."* All free from:
H. J. HEINZ
PO BOX 57
PITTSBURGH, PA 15230

HOT STUFF

If you like your food red hot, you'll definitely want to send for this. *"Tempting Recipes With Red Devil Hot Sauce"* will show you some great ways to spice up your meals. You will also receive a Red Devil discount coupon and a Tabasco catalog. Send a card to:
B. F. TRAPPEY'S SONS. INC.
BOX 400
NEW IBERIA, LA 70560

YAM IT UP

How would you like to enjoy a marshmallow yam dessert or yam orange cookies? These are just two of the tasty treats you'll find featured in the *"Sweet Potato recipe* collection" with dozens of prize winning yam recipes. Free from:
LOUISIANA SWEET POTATO COMMISSION

P.O. Box 113
Opelousas, LA 70571-0113

SHERRY, SHERRY

The makers of the original cream sherry –
Harvey's Bristol Cream have a great recipe col-
lection just for the asking. You'll find Peachy
Cranberry Sauce for pork, Millionaire's Man-
hattan plus lots more. Send a long SASE and
ask for *HBC's Recipes* to:
HBC Recipe Collection
PO Box 767
Holmdel, NJ 07733

SALAD DRESSING

This small collection gives you 5 recipes using
Uncle Dan's Salad Dressing and shows how it
can be used as seasoning, for party dips and
even as a sandwich spread. Write to:
Uncle Dan's
PO Box 980
Yakima, WA 98907

COOKOUTS ARE FUN

Grill Lovers Catalog" has some-
thing every barbecue chef will en-
joy having. Free from:
W. C. Bradley
Box 1240
Columbus, GA 31902.

GARDEN OF EDEN

The fig has been with us ever
since Adam and Eve decided
that fig leaves made nifty ap-
parel. Now *"Buyers Guide To
Dietary Fiber"* along with
*"Fabulous Figs - The Fitness
Fruit"* and *"This Fig Can Teach
You A Lot About Nutrition"* will
give you delicious new ways to use this delight-
ful and nutritious fruit. Free from:
Dried Fruit Advisory Board
Box 709
Fresno, CA 93712

UMMM ... GOOD

Campbell has a special collection of recipes along with a discount coupon waiting for you. They feature their tasty line of soups. When you write ask for the *Golden Corn Soup Chronology.* Write to:
CAMPBELL SOUP CO.
HOME ECONOMICS DEPT.
CAMPBELL PLACE
CAMDEN, NJ 08101

ALMOND SPECIALTIES

For a change of pace try using almonds to flavor your next meal. The *"Fast & Fabulous"* collection will show you how to use almonds in everything from chocolate-almond apricot bread, turkey tetrazzini almondine and almond-blueberry fruit cake. Free from:
ALMOND BOARD OF CALIFORNIA
12TH STREET, BOX 31307
MODESTO, CA 95354

OLIVE OIL RECIPES

When dinner's done you may receive a standing ovation from your family for the meal you just made with the help of this recipe collection. *"How To Change Your Oil & Recipes"* will give you a couple of dozen creative meal ideas using olive oil. You will also receive a store discount coupon. Send a card to:
POMPEIAN OLIVE OIL
4201 PULASKI HIGHWAY
BALTIMORE, MD 21224

"COOKING WITH SWEET POTATOES"

Here's a collection of 28 tasty meals using sweet potatoes. You'll enjoy the main dishes and colorful casseroles featuring sweet potatoes in combination with other vegetables and meats. For your free copy write:
SWEET POTATO COUNCIL
5023 IROQUIS ST.
COLLEGE PARK, MD 20740

SWEET 'N LOW SAMPLES

For an envelope full of Sweet & Low samples

plus a handy carry case, just send a SASE and request *"Sweet & Low Samples."* Send to:
SWEET & LOW, CUMBERLAND PACKING CORP
2 CUMBERLAND ST.
BROOKLYN, NY 11205

CAN IT!

When's the best time to can? What's the best way to preserve flavor when you freeze? A handy newsletter is yours for the asking. There are no recipes but it provides you with tips and a timetable for canning vegetables, meats, and fruits plus advice in seasoning and preserving flavor. Free from:
KERR GLASS MANUFACTURING CORP.
BOX 97
SAND SPRING, OK 74063

FRESH FROM FLORIDA

What a wonderful package this is—an outstanding collection of recipes and information on seafood and aquaculture. Discover how to make a Seafare Saute & lots more. Send a long SASE to:
BOB CRAWFORD
COMMISSIONER OF AGRICULTURE &
CONSUMER SERVICES
BUREAU OF SEAFOOD &
AQUACULTURE
2051 EAST DIRAC DR.
TALLAHASSEE, FL 32310-3760

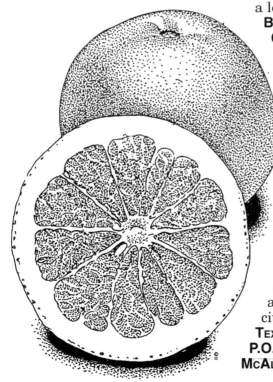

"TEXASWEET CITRUS RECIPES"

This collection of mouth-watering citrus recipes comes to you from TexaSweet. Their Ruby Red grapefruit has a sweet, juicy flavor. The recipes cover breakfast, dinner, dessert and drinks using this delectable citrus. Send a postcard to:
TEXASWEET
P.O. BOX 2497
MCALLEN. TX 78501

BE CREATIVE

The *"Light & Elegant Cookbook"* includes recipes of all kinds with everything from soups to nuts. All these exciting meals feature Lea & Perrins Sauce. There's even a nice index to help you easily find the recipe you want. Free from:
LEE & PERRINS SAUCE
POLLITT DR.
FAIRLAWN, NJ 07410

THOMAS' PROMISES..

If you like Thomas' English Muffins plain—you'll love 'em fancy. To get their *"English Muffins Recipes"* plus a discount coupon, send a postcard to:
S.B. THOMAS. INC.
930 N. RIVERVIEW DR.
TOTOWA, NJ 07512

"NUTRITION FACTS"

Oscar Mayer sandwich spreads are easy and versatile to use. Try the spreads on crackers, breads and in other recipes. For a nice collection of recipe ideas, send a postcard to:
OSCAR MAYER
DEPT. ST, P.O. BOX 7188
MADISON, WI 53707

YOUNG AT HEART

If you are one of the 60 million Americans with high blood pressure, you should learn how to eat right. Send for the free booklet, *"So You Have High Blood Cholesterol"* from:
INFORMATION CENTER
NATIONAL HEART, LUNG, & BLOOD INSTITUTE
7200 WISCONSIN AVE., PO BOX 30105
BETHESDA, MD 20824

NUTS ABOUT NUTS

If you're crazy about nuts, *All The Goodness of Hawaii is* the catalog for you. You can order anything from Macadamia Nuts to Kona Coffee. For your free copy, send a postcard to:

MAUNA LOA
MAINLAND GIFT CENTER
PO BOX 1772
PEORIA, IL 61656

A SWEET WAY TO CHEAT

If you love sweets (and who doesn't) but must watch your weight *"26 Ways To Get Back To Nature"* is for you. For your free copy of this booklet plus four others including *"Cakes For All Occasions"*, send a postcard to:
SUGAR FOODS CORP.
9500 EL DORADO AVE., P.O. BOX 1220
SUN VALLEY CA 91352

CREOLE COOKING

If you enjoy the unique taste and flavors of cajon and creole food, this one's for you. Tony Chachere's Creole Foods, featured in Oprah Winfrey's cookbook *"In The Kitchen With Rosie"* would like to send you a free cookbook showing you how to use their creole seasoning to create old-fashioned Louisiana taste delights. Write to
TONY CHACHERE'S CREOLE FOODS
533 NORTH LOMBARD ST.,
PO BOX 1687
OPELOUSAS, LA 70571

EIGHT FOR DINNER

The American Lamb Council several recipe collections that will show you exciting ways to make your dinners more delightful. The collection includes *Make It Simple, Make It Sizzle,* and *Festive Lamb Recipes,* plus several others. You'll find wine-basted, marinated, grilled, roasted and broiled recipes using fresh American lamb. Send a long SASE to:
THE AMERICAN LAMB COUNCIL
6911 S. YOSEMITE ST.
ENGLEWOOD, CO 80112

BRING HOME THE BACON

If you like bacon, be sure to get your copy of *"Savor The flavor, Round The Clock With Oscar Mayer Bacon."* In it

you'll discover tasty recipes and cooking ideas featuring bacon. They will also include party & cookout recipes using Oscar Mayers Little Wieners & Little Smokies plus Nutrition Facts. Send a postcard to:
BACON BOOKLET
OSCAR MAYER CONSUMER CENTER
PO BOX 7188
MADISON, WI 53707

DELICIOUS SKINNY BEEF

Looking for something easy but delicious for your family's meals? How about meals that are perfect for anyone watching their weight? Try something different... like 'beef, pasta & artichoke toss' or 'quick steak & vegetable soup'. Send a SASE and ask for *Delicious Easy Beef Recipes From Skinny Beef*. Send to:
MEAT BOARD TEST KITCHENS
DEPT. DEBR, 444 N. MICHIGAN AVE
CHICAGO, IL 60611

HOW TO COMFORT

Now you can make some great desserts, drinks even coffee using that versatile liquor from Kentucky — Southern Comfort. If you want more delicious recipe ideas, write:
SOUTHERN COMFORT COMPANY
DEPT. GT, BOX 1080
LOUISVILLE, KY 40201

WINE AND DINE

The Gallo recipe collection will provide you with dozens of palate pleasing ways of using Gallo to enhance your next meal. Included is a delightful recipe for Goumet Pizza and lots more. These recipes will let you turn everyday cooking into an adventure. Write to:
E & J GALLO WINERY
MODESTO, CA 95353

"WHITE WINE RECIPES"

Wine lovers delight in trying new wines and new ways to enjoy familiar wines. With this compact collection of recipes you'll create tasty new meals using the fine wines of Widmer. Free from:

W<small>IDMER</small> W<small>INE</small> C<small>ELLARS</small>
N<small>APLES</small>, NY 14512

WINE LOVERS

"Beaulieu Vineyards" describes and pictures the Beaulieu line of fine wines. Also includes a card for a free wine tasting tour of their vineyard. Write to:
B<small>EAULIEU</small> V<small>INEYARDS</small>
PO B<small>OX</small> 329
R<small>UTHERFORD</small>, CA 94573

VIRGIN ISLAND RUM

Cruzan Rum is an exceptionally clean tasting rum that works well with mixers or on its own. For your copy of the free *"Imported Rum Recipes"*, write:
C<small>RUZAN</small> R<small>UM</small> D<small>ISTILLERY</small>
PO B<small>OX</small> 218, F<small>REDERIKSTED</small>
S<small>T</small>. C<small>ROIS</small>, VI 00840

CORDIAL RECIPES

Hiram Walker has put together a selection of over 30 famous food and drink recipes from around the world. These recipes all feature their fine line of cordials. Just ask for their free *"The Best Of Kahlua"*. Pink Chinchilla Pie anyone? Write to
H<small>IRAM</small> W<small>ALKER</small>
P.O. B<small>OX</small> 33006
D<small>ETROIT</small>, MI 48232

CHAMBORD RECIPES

Chambord is a liqueur made with small black raspberries plus other fruits & herbs combined with honey. For new ways to enjoy this magnificent liqueur send for the free *"Chambord Recipe Book"* from:
C<small>HAMBORD</small> R<small>ECIPES</small>
L<small>A</small> M<small>AISON</small> D<small>ELAN</small> E<small>T</small> C<small>IE</small>
2180 O<small>AKDALE</small> D<small>R</small>.
P<small>HILADELPHIA</small>, PA 19125

For Home & Garden

POTPOURRI BONNETS

These delightful miniature straw hat bonnet magnets are filled with potpourri and ready for your refrigerator or bath room. They are yours for two first class loose stamps. Send to:

VALERIE'S HATTERY
4494 POLK
DEARBORN, MI 48125

HOME SECURITY TIPS

There are many ways to protect your property from burglars. If you don't have a security system in your home, there are still things you can do. The Newent Co., will send you an authentic appearing sample alarm warning sticker along with all kinds of "Home Security Tips." Don't wait, protect yourself and your property from criminals today. Ask for: *Warning Sticker & Security Tips.* Send a SASE to:

THE NEWENT COMPANY NEWSLETTER
PO BOX 40
CANTERBURY, CT 06331

SOLAR ENERGY & YOUR HOME

One day your home may be heated and powered with free energy from the sun. Here are the answers to many of the most frequently asked questions about putting solar and other kinds of renewable energy to work for you. Write to:

RENEWABLE ENERGY INFORMATION
BOX 8900
SILVER SPRINGS, MD 20907

There is a toll-free phone number you can call to get in touch directly with an expert who can answer specific questions you may have about renewable energy. There are also a large num-

ber of free booklets dealing with all aspects of renewable energy available by calling the same 800 number.
Call: **800-523-2929.**

Finally, if you have a computer and modem you can access the Department of Energy and Renewable Resouces, on the Worldwide Web. They even have free software you can download. Their home page is located at: wwweren.doe.gov and their bbs can be reached at:
http://erecbbs.nciinc.com

"TIPS FOR ENERGY SAVERS"

Saving energy not only makes America less energy dependent on other nations - it will save you a tidy sum of money too. The Department of Energy would like you to have a useful energy-saving package. Ask for the *"Energy Saver Booklets."* It's yours free from:
D.O.E. Technical Information Center
Box 62, Oak Ridge, TN 37830

WHAT DOES FIBERGLAS DO?

"All About Insulation" and *"Owens-Corning Fiberglas"* are two of the useful guides found in the "Fiberglas information series". You'll find out how Fiberglas is made and how it's used for insulation, dust-stops and air filters. Free from:
Owen Corning Fiberglas
Fiberglas Tower
Toledo, OH 43659

HOME REMODELING

Are you getting ready to remodel? The "Anderson *Home Remodeling Series"* is a must for you. Your creative juices will begin to flow as you thumb through this beautifully illustrated idea book. The answer book will provide help in solving your remodeling problems whether adding a room or simply changing a window. Write to:
Anderson Corp.
Bayport, MN 55003

IN-SINK ERATOR

If you're considering a garbage disposal, trash compactor or hot water dispenser check out In-Sink Erator. Ask for their *information package* and then decide which is best for your needs and budget. Write:
IN-SINK ERATOR
4700 21ST ST.
RACINE, WI 53406

LET THE SUN SHINE IN

If you're planning on building or remodeling a house, have you thought about which windows and doors are right for you? "Window Scaping" tells all about the many types of windows and doors available to help you to decide for yourself. It's free from:
ROLSCREEN CO.
PELLA, IA 50219

STAIN REMOVAL

This helpful Emergency Spot Removal Guide will help you get rid of some of the trickiest stains you may get on your carpets or draperies. It is free for the asking and will come with discount coupons. Drop a postcard to:
COIT DRAPERY & CARPET CLEANERS
DEPT. ABJ, 897 HINKLEY RD.
BURLINGAME, CA 94010

BEAUTIFY & PROTECT YOUR HOME

Red Devil would like to show you the right way to beautify your home with wall coverings and protect it with caulk. Ask them for the free "wallcovering and caulk booklets." Write to:
RED DEVIL INC.
CONSUMER RELATIONS
PO BOX 3133,
UNION, NJ 07083

"STORY OF HARDWOOD PLYWOOD"

If you are a handyman you will enjoy this informative booklet which gives the whole story of

plywood. Best of all you'll receive a set of 4 different plans showing you how to build a bookcase, room divider, saddle seat desk and TV trays (planter/desk/stereo, etc.) All free from:
HARDWOOD PLYWOOD MANUFACTURERS
PO Box 2789
RESTON, VA 22090

BUILDING A HOUSE

You may still be able to afford the home you've always wanted. For the past quarter century Miles Homes has helped over 15,000 people enjoy home ownership with their step-by-step instructions and pre-cut material. For a free copy of their 80 page *color catalog* with 50 exciting models to choose from, write to:
MILES HOMES
4700 NATHAN LANE
PO Box 41310
MINNEAPOLIS, MN 55442

"SAVE WATER"

Here's a fully illustrated guide on how to pinpoint water waste in your toilet and what to do about it. You'll also receive a sample of the dye used to detect leaks. Drop a postcard to:
FLUIDMASTER
PO Box 4264
1600 VIA BURTON
ANAHEIM, CA 92803

WALLPAPER BY MAIL

This great *catalog* offers you an excellent selection of high quality wall covering products at low prices. To make your selection easier, they will send you free swatches of the paper and even matching fabrics. Send a postcard to:
ROBINSON'S WALLCOVERINGS
225 WEST SPRING ST.
TITUSVILLE, PA 16354

"GUIDE TO PAINT & VARNISH REMOVAL"

In this handy guide you will learn some great and easy ways to improve the appearance of your house. There are quick and easy methods for removing mildew and mildew stains from both interior and exterior surfaces. These helpful hints are a must for any tough cleaning job. Send for your free guide to:

SAVOGRAN COMPANY
P.O. BOX 130
NORWOOD, MA 02062

WORRY-FREE: SEPTIC SYSTEM

If you have a septic system, time may be running out before your system fails. Before that happens, the makers of RID-X would like to send you this informative booklet, which can help you avoid septic system failure. Send a card to:

RID-X
DEPT. MBD
MONTVALE, NJ 07645

AMGARD SECURITY

To protect your family and home, a home security alarm system is essential. To help you decide on what type of protection is best for you and your family ask for the free *Amgard Security Planning Guide.* Drop a card to:

AMGARD SECURITY OFFER
AMWAY CORPORATION-33A-2J
ADA, MI 49355

THE ALL PURPOSE WONDER

Want to save money and look good too? Send for *"This Little Box With A House Full of Uses."* In it you will learn how to use baking soda in ways you never thought of...in the kitchen, bathroom, basement, even on your pet. Write to:

ARM & HAMMER
CONSUMER RELATIONS
CHURCH & DWIGHT CO.
PRINCETON, NJ 08547

"STAIN REMOVAL"

Most stains can be removed by following certain procedures. The people at Maytag have an excellent stain removal guide they will send to you just for the asking. Remember, once you master the steps it's easy to remove just about any stain by referring to this handy guide. You'll also receive *"Facts of Laundry.- Choosing The Right Laundry Additives"* Send a postcard to:

MAYTAG COMPANY
CUSTOMER EDUCATION DEPT.
ONE DEPENDABILITY SQUARE
NEWTON, IA 50208

CARPET CLEANING

Hoover will send you a free guide to carpet care. The "Consumer Guide to Carpet Cleaning" is loaded with carpet care tips and facts, cleaning alternatives , a stain removal chart and more. This 16 page booklet provides important information you should know. Ask for *"Consumer Guide to Carpet Cleaning."* SASE to:

THE HOOVER COMPANY
CONSUMER EDUCATION, DEPT. FC
101 E. MAPLE ST.
NORTH CANTON, OH 44720

SLIP-FREE BATHTUB

If you've always wanted to have a slip-free bathtub, here's your chance. You'll never have to use messy bathtub stick-ems or a rubber mat. The makers of Trusty Step have great news for you...a simple 3 minute treatment can make your tub slip-free forever. Send a SASE to:

TRUSTY STEP
405 TARRYTOWN RD. SUITE 414
WHITE PLAINS, NY 10607

FREE ANTI-TARNISH BAGS

If you would like to keep your silverware shining like new, try storing it in Hagerty's Tarnish Intercept Bags. Once the silverware is placed inside and the bag zipper is closed, it locks out tarnish. The inside of the bag will blacken when it has absorbed all the corrosion-causing gases. You then remove the silver and place it in a new bag. For free samples of the tarnish intercept bag, write to:

W. J. HAGERTY SONS, LTD.
P.O. BOX 1496
SOUTH BEND, IN 46624.
OR FOR ANSWERS TO YOUR QUESTIONS ABOUT TARNISHING, CALL: **1-800-348-5162 x137**

STAIN OUT HOTLINE

Do you have questions about problem stains on those favorite garments What do you do if it's an unknown mystery stain and you don't know where to begin? The Dow Stain Experts, the makers of Spray'N Wash, have the answers for you. Give them a call at:
1-800 260-1066

SHINGLE IT

Lots of remodeling ideas are contained in this great *Red Shingle & Shake package.* It shows how to use shingles and shakes outside and inside your house. These guides also show how to do-it-yourself and save. Drop a card to:
RED CEDAR SHINGLE & HANDSPLIT SHAKE BUREAU
SUITE 275, 515 116TH AVE. N.E.
BELLEVUE, WA 98004

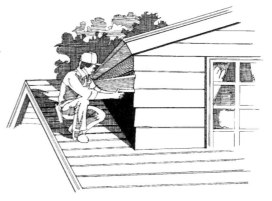

COLORS & CLOROX

Here are lots of helpful tips from Clorox on keeping your clothes clean, bright and stain free. Ask for *"Emergency Spot Removal Guide."* Drop a card to:
THE CLOROX CO.
PO BOX 24305
OAKLAND, CA 94623

CHOOSING CARPETING

Dupont Company offers you this free booklet *"Consumer's Guide To Choosing Carpets"* to help answer all your questions about carpet care.

Drop a card to:
DUPONT CO.
ROOM G 40284
WILMINGTON, DE 19898.

LIGHT UP YOUR GARDEN

Like to add a colorful look to your garden? Consider using Holland or domestic bulbs. For a full color catalog write to:
VAN BOURGONDIEN
PO BOX A, 245 FARMINGDALE RD.
ROUTE 109
BABYLON, NY 11702

BURPEE GARDENS

This catalog is packed with everything you can imagine to start your vegetable, flower or fruit garden. They have seed starter kits and plants. You'll even find garden helpers, bird houses and fun seed kits for kids. Grow your own herb garden right on your kitchen window sill. When you call or write mention *OFFER #82* and in addition to their new *Flowering Bulb and Perennial Catalogue*, you'll also receive a special $5.00-off coupon. Free from:
W. ATLEE BURPEE & CO.
WARMINSTER, PA 18974
OR CALL 1-800-888-1447

WHY PLANTS FAIL

The question of why some plants fail to grow even when they are carefully tended to, has always been somewhat of a mystery. Now Gurney Seed and Nursery would like to throw some light on the subject so you can have a more beautiful garden. They will also send you the new *Gurney Catalog*. It features over 4000 items—many shown in full color. You'll find how-to-grow-it tips plus planting charts and moisture guides along with many special offers. If you'd like a packet of giant sunflower seeds, include a quarter. Write:
GURNEY SEED & NURSERY CO.

DEPT. 84, 1130 PAGE ST.
YANKTON SD 57079

GO ORGANIC

"How To Grow An Organic Garden"
will get you started raising your
own delicious and naturally
pure vegetables. It even includes a plan for a sample garden. Get your free copy and let
Mother Nature do her thing.
Write to:
ORGANIC GARDENING & FARMING
33 E. MINOR ST.
EMMAUS, PA 18049

GROWING IDEAS

In the last few years backyard community gardens have been popping up all over the nation.
Bring your community together and save money
too - start a community garden. You'll also receive teaching tools to help young minds grow.
Ask for the free *"Growing Ideas"* from:
NATIONAL GARDEN ASSOCIATION
180 FLYNN AVE.
BURLINGTON, VT 05401

EXOTIC IMPORTED PLANTS

If you enjoy unusual and out-of-the ordinary type plants this one's for you. The new *Stokes seed catalog* features 1300 varieties including many imported from England, Europe, and Canada. Get your free catalog from:
STOKES SEEDS INC.
BOX 548
BUFFALO, NY 14240

MILLER'S NURSERY GUIDE

In this new catalog you'll find a new seedless grape, virus-free berries and several pages of tested recipes and a whole lot more. Miller Nurseries has put together a broad selection of their most popular nursery items. Ask for their new *Catalog & Planting Guide*:
J. E. MILLER NURSERIES
DEPT. 706
WEST LAKE RD.
CANAN-DAIGUA, NY 14424

LAWN CARE

Here's a super 5-star special for anyone with a lawn or garden. To help improve lawn, flowers, vegetable garden, trees and shrubs - call the experts at Scott Lawn Products on their toll-free phone. They have the answers to any and all questions about lawn growing, disease, fertilizing, problem areas etc. They'll give you a free subscription to *"Lawn Care"* with loads of useful information (plus money saving coupons). They'll be happy to send you any of the dozens of booklets, magazines and brochures that will help you grow the perfect lawn or garden. Excellent. Call toll free:
(800) 543-TURF OR WRITE:
SCOTT LAWN PRODUCTS
14111 SCOTTS LAWN RD.
MARYVILLE, OH 43041

FULL-SIZE FRUIT FROM DWARF-SIZE TREES

If your yard is too small to grow as many

fruit trees as you'd like, take a look at this free catalog. These dwarf trees grow only 8 to 10 feet tall but grow full size apples, peaches, pears, cherries, and nectarines. This catalog features almost 400 varieties of fruit, shade and nut trees plus shrubs, vines, ornamentals, and award-winning roses. Send a postcard for the catalog and special offers to:

STARK BROTHER NURSERIES & ORCHARD CO.
BOX A12119
LOUISIANA, MO 63353

FREE FERTILIZER

Free manure is available to gardeners through Extension Services located throughout the country. To find the one nearest you, call your local U.S. Department of Agriculture Extension Service.

GREAT GARDENS

The Burreil Seed Growers have a nice seed catalog every home gardener will want to have. Before you get ready to plant your next garden be sure to get a copy of this catalog. Send a postcard to:

D.V. BURREIL SEED GROWERS
PO BOX 150H
ROCKY FORD, CO 81067

GARDENER'S HANDBOOK

If you want to learn how to have a beautiful fruitful garden, be sure to get a free copy of *"The Park Gardener's Handbook."* In it you will find all kinds of useful information that will help you to get more productive results from your gardening efforts. You can also choose from over 3000 new and rare varieties of flowers and vegetables as well as the more familiar types—all available in the full color Park catalog you'll receive. Send a postcard to:

GEORGE **W.** PARK SEED CO. INC.
254 COKEBURY ROAD
GREENWOOD, **SC 29647**

Stay Healthy

CHILD SAFETY

Hidden Hazards II spotlights potential family safety risks. Every parent is interested in the safety of their child and the products that are around that are safe and hazardous. Ask for Hidden Hazards II. For your free copy, send a SASE to:

COALITION FOR CONSUMER HEALTH AND SAFETY
PO BOX 12099
WASHINGTON, DC 20005-0999

BREAST FEEDING GUIDE

If you are a new mother or soon to be one, this handy *Breast Feeding Guide* will answer most of the questions you may have about breast feeding. Write for this excellent information to:

MEDELA, INC.
PO BOX 660
MC HENRY, IL 60051-0660

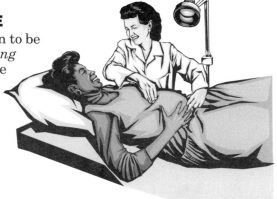

EAR INFECTIONS

Anyone with a child knows the trauma involved when the child suffers an earache. Learn the causes, symptoms and cures of ear infections before the suffering begins. This handy guide will explain everything. Ask for:

A PARENT'S GUIDE TO CHILDREN'S EARACHE
c/o CHILDREN'S TYLENOL
1675 BROADWAY, 33RD FL.
NEW YORK, NY 10019

CHOLESTEROL & BLOOD PRESSURE

Call the National Heart, Lung and Blood Institute for recorded information on cholesterol and high blood pressure. When you call leave your name and address for written information. Call:
1-800-575-WELL

HOLISTIC HERBAL HEALTHCARE GUIDE

This herbal guide will give you basic information about herbs, herbal combinations and homeopathic medicines. You'll learn the five main benefits of herbs, why people use herbs, what herbs are sources of vitains, minerals and trace minerals and important points that should be considered when purchasing herbs for personal consumption. If you would like a copy of *The Holistic Herbal Healthcare Guide,* send your name, address and 4 first class stamps to cover postage to:

DEBORAH COBLE
1420-E3 STEEPLE CHASE DRIVE
DOVER, PA 17315-3784

YOUR HEART

The American Heart Association. Your call will be routed to your local AHA office for information on heart disease, strokes, high blood pressure and diet. Some offices can tell you about local support groups or low-cost or free screenings for blood pressure and cholesterol. Call:
1-800-AHA-USA-1

YOUNG AT HEART

The National Institute on Aging would like you to have a copy of *"For Hearts and Arteries: What Scientists are Learning About Age and the Cardiovascular System."* Learn how the latest research can help keep your heart running younger no matter what your age.
NIA INFORMATION CENTER
PO BOX 8057
GAITHERSBURG, MD. 20898-8057
OR CALL **1-800-222-2225**

DISCOVER THE WORLD OF NATURAL MEDICINE

If you are interested in learning about natural remedies and natural products and their effect on your body send for this *catalog of homeopathic remedies.* Enzymatic Therapy and Leaning offer you some of their natural methods of feeling

better. They will even send you a $3.00 coupon to try Herpilyn, a cold sore remedy. To get answers to your questions, you can call their consumer information line.
1-800-783-2286

BIOFEEDBACK

Did you ever wonder how those people who do the research on reward gratification process works. Today's alternative methods of treating people include "Biofeedback," (when you accomplish something you're given a reward). Learn more about these techniques and how they make us healthy and happier. For information about certified biofeedback professionals, send a letter and SASE to:
BIOFEEDBACK CERTIFICATION INSTITUTE OF AMERICA
10200 W. 44TH AVE., SUITE 304
WHEAT RIDGE, CO 80033

TENSION & DEPRESSION

The National Mental Health Association has lots of information on how to handle tension and depression. If you have any questions, they have a toll- free number and will send you helpful information. Call:
THE NATIONAL MENTAL HEALTH ASSOCIATION,
ALEXANDRIA, VA
1-800-969-6642

TEEN SMOKING

Centers for Disease Control's Offices on Smoking and Health will help you tackle questions on how to curb teen smoking. For specific advice, call:
1-800-CDC-1311

KEEPING YOUR HEART HEALTHY

The American Heart Association has a toll-free helpline. Calling that helpline, you can get free copies of a host of booklets dealing with your heart. Topics include blood pressure, CPR, cholesterol, diet, exercise, heart disease and strokes to mention just a few. Learn the best ways to eat smart and healthy by reducing fat in your diet. You can also learn you how to read the new food labels to help you shop for healthier foods. Ask for *"How to Read the New Food Label,"* and *"Save Food Dollars and Help Your Heart"* and for any other heart-related topics you are interested in. Write to:

THE AMERICAN HEART ASSOCIATION
NATIONAL CENTER
7272 GREENVILLE AVE.
DALLAS, TX 75231.
OR CALL:1-800-242-8721

SLEEP HOTLINE

The American Society of Travel Agents and Searle Provide tips on how to feel your best while traveling. Request a free brochure titled *"Sleep Well... Stay Fit - Tips for Travelers."*
1-800-SHUTEYE

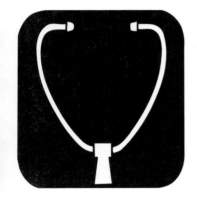

NATIONAL CANCER INSTITUTE

To help you keep informed about the most up-to-date information about cancer, the National Cancer Institute has a toll-free number you can call. When you call you can ask for free publications, or ask for help locating FDA-approved mammography facilities or talk with cancer specialists.
1-800-422-6237

JOINT REPLACEMENT

If you or anyone you know ever needs joint replacement you will want to read this valuable information. You will learn Why and when it is necessary... how it is performed.. benefits...risks. Ask for: *"Total Joint Replacement."* Send a SASE to:

AMERICAN ACADEMY OF ORTHOPEDIC SURGEONS
BOX 2058
DES PLAINES, IL 60016

BLADDER PROBLEMS

Did you know that nearly half a milliom people suffer from interstitial cystitis an often misdiagnosed chronic bladder disorder. The National Institutes of Health has published a free booklet that gives basic information in layuman's terms on the disease. Ask for "Interstitial Cystitis" by writing to:

IC Booklet
National Kidney and Urologic Diseases
Information Clearinghouse
3 Information Way
Bethesda, MD. 20892-3580

THE FACTS ABOUT PROSTATE CANCER

"Early Detection of Prostate Cancer" answers the most often -asked questions about prostate cancer. Although the disease is of prime concern to men over 55, it explains that the disease can often exist without symptoms and that men over 40 should tested annually. The National Cancer Institute also includes a list of problems that might indicate prostate cancer. It also covers the specifics of diagnosis, treatment, and prognosis- which is excellent if the condition is caught early enough. For your free copy or to speak with a specialist call:
1-800-422-6237

CANCER HOTLINE

The National Cancer Institute's Information Service provides the latest information about cancer, including causes and medical referral to low-cost clinics, medical consultation, referral to patient support groups and publications on request. They can provide you with literature and answer questions concerning various types of cancer and the standard treatment. Send a postcard to:

NCI, Cancer Information Service
NCI Building 31, Room 10A1B
Bethesda, MD 20205
or call **1-800-4-CANCER**

"A HEALTHIER YOU"

Research shows that eating fresh fruits and vegetables help put more fiber in your diet and helps make for a healthier you. Information about the vitamins, minerals and fiber in fruits and vegetables are essential to a healthier you.

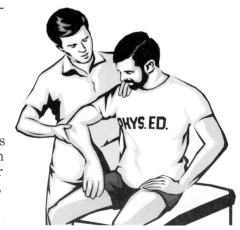

This booklet from the American Institute for Cancer Research includes healthy recipes. Just send a SASE to:

THE AMERICAN INSTITUTE FOR CANCER RESEARCH
DEPT. AP
WASHINGTON, DC 20069

BACK TROUBLES?

The BackSaver catalog has a wonderful assortment of all types of products for your back, including chairs, seat and back support cushions, sleeping supports, reading tables and more. It's free from:

BACKSAVER PRODUCTS CO.
53 JEFFREY AVE.
HOLLISTON, MA 01746

WHAT EVERY NOSE KNOWS

If you are one of the 60 million Americans who suffer from nasal and sinus congestion, sinusitis and allergies, this kit's for you. The American Lung Association and Tavis-D have developed *"The T.E.S.T.- Tavis Exam For Sinus Treatment."* To receive a free "Allergy Management Kit,"

CALL **1-800-828-4783**

HEAR THIS

If you are experiencing hearing loss and your doctor has recommended a hearing aid, you may need help in determining what kind of device you need. The American Speech -Language-Hearing Association, offers general information about hearing aids and their costs, insurance coverage, proper fit and care. For your free copy *"How to Buy a Hearing Aid,"*

CALL **1-800-638-8255**

PARENT RESOURCE GUIDE

It's important for children to develop good eating habits when they are young so that they can grow up to be healthier , more active adults. The American Academy of Pediatrics has some important nutrition information just for the asking. Send a business sized SASE to:

NUTRITION BROCHURES DEPT., C
AMERICAN ACADEMY OF PEDIATRICS
PO Box 927
ELK GROVE, IL 60009

ALLERGIES AND ASTHMA

If you have questions about allergies or asthma, here's how you can find answers. The Asthma and Allergy Foundation will answer any questions you have regarding the symptoms of allergies to different substances, foods and how all these can be related to asthma.
CALL: **1-800-7-ASTHMA**

ABC'S OF EYECARE

The Better Vision Institute has some worthwhile information on your eyes and how to take the best care of them. Topics include everything from the proper selection of eyeglass frames, to eye care for children & adults, tips on correct lighting, correct type of sunglasses and more. Send a business-sized SASE to:

BETTER VISION INSTITUTE
PO Box 77097
WASHINGTON, DC 20013
OR CALL **1-800-424-8422**

DEPRESSION AWARENESS

Today we are very aware of everything around us and yet we sometimes blot out or deny the signs of depression in ourselves and those around us. This very informative information on depression is published by the National Institute of Mental Health. Learn all the facts and become aware. Send a business-sized, SASE to:

D/ART, NIMH
5600 FISHERS LANE, ROOM. 10-85
ROCKVILLE, MD 20857
OR CALL: **1-800-421-4211**

HEALTHY TEETH

Teeth: we get one set of permanent healthy adult teeth so it's essential to learn how to keep them strong and cavity free. Dental care is also a very important career opportunity that also allows you to help others take care of their teeth. If you think you may be interested in finding out more about career options, ask for a copy of *Dental Hygiene - A Profession of Opportunities* and also *Facts About Dental Hygiene*. Send a SASE to:

AMERICAN DENTAL HYGIENISTS' ASSOCIATION
444 N. MICHIGAN AVE.
CHICAGO, IL 60611
ATTN: NUTRITION DEPT.

WELLNESS GUIDE FOR OLDER ADULTS

The purpose of this *Wellness Guide* is to offer you advice on health issues and preventive care. It is designed to provide practical information on matters such as sensory changes, diet, exercise, legal and financial matters as well as common health problems - all designed to help you remain vibrant, active and independent throughout life. Write to:

MARKETING SERVICES
PENNSYLVANIA HOSPITAL
800 SPRUCE STREET
PHILADELPHIA, PA 19107

MIND OVER BODY

This informative resource directory comes to you from The Institute Of Noetic Sciences. Learn just how powerful our minds can be in controlling our bodies and how the mind can help us heal ourselves.

CALL TOLL-FREE: **1-800-628-4545**

HYSTERECTOMY

The American College of Obstetricians and Gynecologists has published a free pamphlet *"Un-*

derstanding Hysterectomy" which outlines what constitutes a medically necessary hysterectomy and describes what the surgery involves. Request a copy, it's free. Write:
ACOG
409 12TH ST. SW
WASHINGTON, DC 20024

BRAIN FOOD
The brain affects all your vital body functions. If we don't nourish it and exercise it like any other organ it becomes dull. If you want more information on feeding and energizing the brain with the Brain III Formula, call:
1- 800-NU-BRAIN

HIKING SAFETY
Whether you are walking to lose weight, exploring a tourist attraction, or hiking to enjoy scenic trails, there are a number of guideline your should follow. Send a SASE and ask for *"Hiking Safety"* from:
AMERICAN HIKING SOCIETY
DEPT T, PO BOX 20160
WASHINGTON, DC 20041

"MEGABRAIN"
Now you can actually improve your creativity, enhance mental functioning, induce deep relaxation and reduce stress. Sounds amazing but it can be done through the use of a complete line of DAVID light and sound devices, there is even a special application to improve sports performance. To get your free information on this amazing device write:
COMPTRONIC DEVICES LIMITED
9860A 33RD AVENUE
EDMONTON, ALBERTA, CANADA, T6N 1C6

"REV UP"
"Rev Up" is an herbal energy capsule that will help you handle the pressures, deadlines and overloads in your life. The ancient civilizations believed that natural herbs worked wonders for you, and today there seems to be a lot of

merit to those old ideas. Learn all about this personal fatigue fighter and also get a 15% discount.
CALL **800-63-REV-UP**

PARALIMINAL TAPES

Unlike subliminals, Para-liminal Tapes use a unique method of confusing the brain by providing different messages for the right brain and the left brain. This, they fell can help you get you either learn a subject you are interested in or rapidly achieve a goal you've set for yourself. There are 22 unique Paraliminal Tapes. To learn the difference between subliminal and paraliminal, call for your free catalog today:
800-735-TAPE

MASSAGE THERAPY

Stress got you down? The massage therapy booklet will give you detailed information about different methods of massage and benefits of each. It will also answer some of your questions. Write:
AMERICAN MASSAGE THERAPY ASSOCIATION
820 DAVIS ST., SUITE 100
EVANSTON, IL 60201

ASTHMA RELIEF

Asthma patients who use inhalers may be masking the physical cause for their symptoms. Doctors have come up with a checklist for asthma patients who rely on those inhalers to open their airways. If you use the inhaler more than three times a week, if you go through more than one canister a month, and if your asthma awakens you at night, you may be suffering from an inflammation of the airways that is the real cause of your symptoms and may need drug treatment to clear it up. To receive a copy of the list, write to:
ASTHMA INFORMATION CENTER
BOX 790
SPRINGHOUSE, PA 19477

NUTRITION HOTLINE

Find out how your diet is affecting your health. Call the American Institute for Cancer Re-

search, Nutrition Hotline and ask a registered dietician your personal questions on diet, nutrition and cancer. When you call you can leave your question with an operator and a dietician will call you back within 48 hours with an answer to your question.
CALL BETWEEN 9AM -5PM, EST MONDAY-FRIDAY:
1-800-843-8114

FREE HEALTH PUBLICATIONS

The AICR also has a variety of free publications detailed to help you live a healthier lifestyle. A small contribution gets you a very informative newsletter and you can ask for the following booklets by name: *"Get Fit, Trim Down"* - lose weight sensibly. *"Alcohol and Cancer Risk: Make the Choice For Health"*. - find out how alcohol affects your cancer risk. *"Diet & Cancer"* - are you eating enough fiber, something that's been linked to lower cancer risk? *"Reducing Your Risk of Colon Cancer"* - learn steps you can take that may reduce your risk of one of the most common cancers in the United States. Also ask for *"Everything Doesn't Cause Cancer"* which will calm many of the concerns you may have about what causes cancer. You can ask for one of these or all. Write to:
AMERICAN INSTITUTE FOR CANCER RESEARCH
WASHINGTON, DC 20069

HOME HEALTH

This Home Health catalog is the official supplier of Edgar Cayce products for health, beauty and wellness. You'll find over 50 products to help you feel and look your best. There is everything from juices, vitamins, even minerals and salts from the Dead Sea. Write to:
HOME HEALTH
949 SEAHAWK CIRCLE
VIRGINIA BEACH, VA 23452

FREE CHILD'S HEALTH RECORD

This easy to use health record log is great for parents and kids alike. Keep your child's vital health records in this handy easy-to-read log. With it you will keep track of illnesses, allergies, health exams, immunizations and tests,

family history and health insurance, It features the ever popular peanuts gang (Charlie Brown, Snoopy and friends) and is sure to be popular with the little ones. Ask for *"Your Child's Health Record"*. Send a long SASE to:
MET LIFE INSURANCE (16UV)
BOX HR
ONE MADISON AVE.
NEW YORK, NY 10010

IRON - ESSENTIAL MINERAL

In order to understand the effect that iron and iron deficiency on health development of your baby, this free brochure on iron from Carnation, makers of Good Start Infant Formula, and Follow-Up Formula can answer those questions. Ask for: *Iron Brochure*. You'll also learn that although iron is essential for your baby, it is just as essential to a mature adult. Send a SASE to:
CARNATION NUTRITIONAL PRODUCTS
IRON BROCHURE OFFER
PO BOX 65785
SALT LAKE CITY, UT 84165

FAMILY HEALTH RECORD

Every member of the family should keep a medical record. The family's medical record will be useful to you in filling out insurance forms, as well as school and travel records. It can also be vital in helping a physician diagnose a medical problem a family member might have. If you would like they will also send you information on prenatal & natal care, guide to healthy pregnancy and information on how your baby grows. They also have informative brochures for teens about drugs and sexually transmitted disease. Write to:
MARCH OF DIMES
1275 MAMARONECK AVE.
WHITE PLAINS, NY 10605

VISUALLY HANDICAPPED

A great series of publications are free to those with Impaired vision. Printed in very large type are instructions for knitting, crocheting, gardening, children's books, etc. Also available are guides for the partially sighted including a dial operator personal directory. There are also 2 free newsletters—*"IN FOCUS"* for youths and *"SEEING CLEARLY"* for adults. For a complete listing write:

NATIONAL ASSOCIATION FOR VISUALLY HANDICAPPED
305 E. 24TH ST.
NEW YORK, NY 10010
(IN CALIF. ONLY—**3201 BALBOA ST., SAN FRANCISCO, CA 94121).**

JOHNSON & JOHNSON HOTLINE

Who can a consumer turn to for answers to their questions concerning hygiene, personal care and baby care? To help you with these questions Johnson & Johnson has set up a toll-free consumer information hotline you can call. Call them with your questions Monday thru Friday between the hours of from 8:00am to 6:00pm EST.

THEIR TOLL-FREE HOTLINE IS:
1-800-526-3967

CLEAN BILL OF HEALTH

HEARING LOSS

"Straight Talk About Hearing Loss," is a fact-filled book about hearing loss and hearing aids. If you're concerned about hearing loss, get the facts about Miracle-Ear. For your free book CALL: **1-800-582-2911**

HEAR THIS

If you are experiencing hearing loss and your doctor has recommended a hearing aid, you may need help determining what kind of listening device suits you. The American Speech-Language-Hearing Association, offers general information about hearing aids and their costs, insurance coverage, proper fitting and care. They can also make referrals to certified audiologists and speech-language pathologists. To get your free copy ask for *"How to Buy a Hearing Aid,"* CALL **800-638-8255**

HELP FOR THE DEAF

Every year over 200,000 children are born deaf or suffer hearing loss in their first years of life. *"Speech and Hearing Checklist"* tells parents how to detect possible deafness in their children. Another nice booklet, "Listen! Hear!" is for parents of children who may be deaf or hard of hearing. Both are free from:
ALEXANDER GRAHAM BELL ASSOCIATION FOR THE DEAF
3417 VOLTA PL. N.W.
WASHINGTON, **DC 20007**

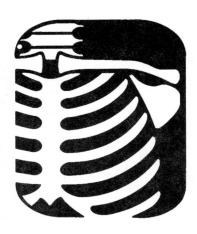

HEALTHY BONES

Supplements can help replace calcium that the years take away. Just two of these soft chewy, vanilla-flavored squares give you 1200 mg of calcium daily. For more information on keeping your bones healthy and staying fit, call toll free weekdays between 9:00am and 5:00pm EST:
1-800-STAY-FIT

BEDWETTER

"Bedwetting— What It's All About and How To End It" is a report written by two medical doctors that will help you end this serious problem before it causes complicated psychological problems. Send a postcard to:
CASE DIRECTION CENTER
555 BIRCH ST.
NEKOOSA, **WI 54457**

FREE MEDICAL SUPPLY CATALOG

You can order your medical supplies from your home by phone and save up to 60%. Send for this free catalog from America's leading mail order medical supply catalog. Drop a postcard to:
BRUCE MEDICAL SUPPLY
DEPARTMENT 712
411 WAVERLY OAKS RD.
WALTHAM. **MA 02154**

FAMILY PLANNING ASSISTANCE

For years Planned Parenthood has provided im-

portant information dealing with making intelligent family planning decisions. Ask for *"Planned Parenthood Guide," "Your Contraceptive Choices"* and *"Sex & Disease - What You Need To Know."* Send a card to:
PLANNED PARENTHOOD
810 7TH AVE.
NEW YORK. NY 10019

INFANT CARE HOTLINE

Being a new parent can be quite unsettling. Now there is someone you can call for help. Beech Nut Baby Foods has set up a toll-free hotline you can call. You will receive expert advice on infant care from a pediatrician, child psychologist, dentist or nutritionist. If you are about to have a child or have recently had one be sure to ask for the *"new parent packet"* and also for information about their label-saving program where you can exchange product UPC labels for discount coupons. Call between the hours of 9am and 8pm E.S.T. weekdays:
1-800-523-6633

MEDICARE HOTLINE

If you have questions or problems regarding Medicare, now there's a toll-free number you can call for help. When you call you can get additional information regarding a Medicare claim you may have, general information about Medicare and the services it provides. They can also help you with information regarding insurance supplements to Medicare, mammograms and lots more. Call:
1-800-638-6833

SURGERY QUESTIONS

If you are considering having any type of non-emergency surgery, be sure to get your free copy of *"Questions to Ask Your Doctor Before Surgery."* It will help you be informed about the options and risks involved. Call toll-free:
1-800-358-9295

SEXUALLY TRANSMITTED DISEASES HOTLINE

If you suspect you may have contracted a sexually transmitted disease, there's a toll free hotline you can call for help and for information. Their specialists will answer your questions concerning STDs and tell you the symptoms that are the warning signals of the disease and how to get help if you need it. You'll be referred to free or low-cost public health clinics or doctors in your area. They would also be happy to send you free brochures concerning STDs. You can call 5 days a week between 8AM and 8PM. Call:
1-800-227-8922

HIV & AIDS HOTLINE

If you have or suspect you may have contracted HIV, there's a toll-free number you can call in confidence for help and for information concerning HIV and AIDS. Call:
1-800-342-2437

VISION AND COMPUTER OPERATORS

Is there any connection between operating a video display terminal and serious eye problems like cataracts? What can be done to reduce the headaches and blurred vision that many computer operators get from staring at a VDT? For answers, send a SASE for "Vision and the VDT Operator." Write to:
AMERICAN OPTOMETRIC ASSOCIATION.
243 N. LINDBERG BLVD.
ST. LOUIS, MO 63141

HEART DIET

If you would like a copy of the American Heart Association recommendations including lists of good and bad foods, and practical suggestions for cutting out the bad stuff. Ask for "Exercise Your Heart," "An Eating Plan For Healthy Americans," "Cholesterol & Your Heart" and "Recipes For Low-Fat, Low Cholesterol Meals." Send a SASE to:
AMERICAN HEART ASSOCIATION, NATIONAL CENTER
PO BOX UCB

7320 Greenville Ave.
Dallas, TX 78531

HELP FOR ALCOHOLICS

Alcoholism is a disease and can be cured. AA wants to help anyone who has (or suspects they have) a drinking problem. Find out what AA is and how it can help - ask for their "information package." All literature comes in an unmarked envelope. Write to:

A A., Box 459
Grand Central Station
New York, NY 10163

SKIN PROTECTION

Prevention is always far better than a cure. For a free booklet *"Skin Cancer: If You Can Spot It You Can Stop It,"* send a long SASE to:

The Skin Cancer Foundation
Box 561
New York, NY 10156

STROKES

For up-to-date information on strokes and effective treatment and therapy for those who fall victim to a stroke, ask for your free copy of *"Guide To Strokes,"* write:

Stroke
NINCDS-W
9000 Rockville Pike, Bldg 31, Rm 8A16
Bethesda, MD 20892

GUIDES TO HEALTHY LIVING

America's pharmaceutical companies would like you to have their *Guides To Healthy Living.* The subjects covered include breast cancer, heart attacks, strokes, menopause, and prostate cancer. For information on any or all of these topics call this information hotline toll-free:

1-800-862-5110

GET FIT !

As part of a program initiated by the President's Council on Physical Fitness and Sports, The Hershey Company has a number of helpful and informative resources that are free for the asking. They are geared to young people ages 6-17. There's even a motivational message from Arnold Schwarzenegger. Learn how to get in shape to meet the presidents challenge. A few of the free items include:

Hershey's Field of Fun - helpful tips for running a field day at school, camp or any other group program.

Official Rule Book of Hershey's Track & Field New Softball Rules

National Track & Field Youth Program - information about this great program including rules and regulations.

The Story Behind The Chocolate Bar - The Story of Milton S. Hershey.

Send a long SASE to:

HERSHEY'S YOUTH PROGRAM
HERSHEYS CHOCOLATE
19 EAST CHOCOLATE AVE.
PO BOX 814
HERSHEY, PA 17033

FREE CONTACT LENSES

If you wear contact lenses or are thinking of getting them, Johnson & Johnson would like you to try their Acuvue contacts. They will send you a certificate good for a free pair of Acuvue contact lenses. To get your free pair, call:
1-800-701-6100

HEALTH HOTLINES

To help answer various health questions you may have there are a number of toll-free hotlines you can call:

CALCIUM INFORMATION CENTER:
1-800-321-2681
MILK CONSUMER HOTLINE:
1-800-WHY-MILK
NATIONAL CENTER FOR NUTRITION & DIURETICS
1-800-366-1655
NATIONAL OSTEOPEROSIS FOUNDATION
1-800-223-9994
FOOD ALLERGY NETWORK
1-800-929-4040
CONSUMER NUTRITION HOTLINE
1-800-366-1655

For Kids

FREE CIRCUS TICKETS

If your child was born in the U.S. last year, he or she is entitled to a free ticket to a Ringling Brothers & Barnum & Bailey Show redeemable any time in his/her lifetime. To get their free ticket parents only need send their newborn's name, address, and date of birth to:

RINGLING BROTHERS & BARNUM & BAILEY
PO Box 39845
EDINA, MN 55439

COMIC BOOK

The American Cancer Society would love to send you a free SpiderMan comic book. SpiderMan and his webbed buddies battle the evil villain Smokescreen in a vivid, and exciting antismoking comic. To get this free comic book ask for the *Spiderman Comic Book.* Call The American Cancer Society at:

1-800-227-2345

FREE COLORING BOOK

If you've ever wanted to know more about your lungs, and have fun while doing it this free offer is for you. You have your choice of three books, an activity book, a coloring book, or a crossword puzzle book. Specify the books you want or ask for the *"facts about smoking"* package: *Smoking...Lungs At Work* #0840; *Second-Hand Smoke; Let's Solve The Smokeword* puzzle-book, #0043. Send it on a postcard to:

AMERICAN LUNG ASSOCIATION
Box 596
NEW YORK, NY 10116

MONEY MANAGEMENT FOR TEENAGERS

Consumer Federation of America has a helpful guide that will help you to teach your teenager

responsible money management. This is a must for every parent. Send a SASE to:
CONSUMER FEDERATION OF AMERICA
"TEACHING YOUR CHILD HOW TO SAVE AND SPEND"
1424 16TH ST. NW, SUITE 604
WASHINGTON, DC 20036

"SCIENCE WEEKLY"

An introduction to the wonderful world of science. Science Weekly, will send you a free sample copy of their newsletter- written specifically for kids. It's an easy read and touches on important topics involving science and is written for kids (grades K - 8th) in order to bring them a better understanding of the sciences, languages and even mathematics. Write and specify which grade level you want when you write to:
SCIENCE WEEKLY
SUBSCRIPTION DEPT.
PO BOX 70154
WASHINGTON, DC 20088

YO YO TRICKS

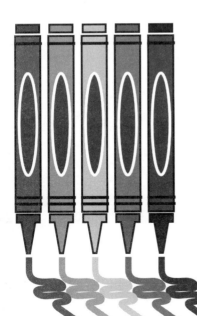

This easy to understand, illustrated pamphlet teaches you the "ancient -art" of *Yo Yo Trickery."* Learn some of the same tricks that made the Yo Yo famous, like Walking the Dog, the Spinner, The Creeper, Loop the Loop and lots more. You'll be learning the fun tournament tricks in no time. Ask for "Yo *Yo Trick Pamphlet."* Send a SASE to:
DUNCAN TOYS CO.
PO BOX 5
MIDDLEFIELD, OH 44062

FREE COLORING BOOKS

The makers of Triaminic cough and cold medicines is giving away two free educational coloring books. These two books are great and help kids to learn and understand about illnesses such as Alzheimer's, epilepsy and diabetes. They offer descriptions and excellent explanations. Ask for:
Kid's Educational Coloring Books. Write to:
JEFF'S COMPANION ANIMAL SHELTER

c/o Sandoz Pharmaceuticals
59 Route 10
E. Hanover, NJ 07936

OWLIE SKYWARN

What can you do to make yourself safe from lightning, tornadoes and hurricanes? Owlie Skywarn has two freebies you will want to have:
1. *"Hurricanes & Tornados* - tells about the causes and devastating effects of storms, hurricanes and tornados.
2. "Owlie Skywarn Weather Book" - learn exactly what weather is and what causes the changes in seasons.
For your free copies write:
National Logistics Support Center
1510 East Bannister Rd. Bldg. #1
Kansas City, MO 64131

MAKE A BUTTON

This great kit is not only fun but can be a profit-maker too. If you like collecting buttons, you'll love making your own. Send for your *free catalog and free idea book* today. Drop a card to:
Badge A Minit
348 North 30th Rd.
La Salle, IL 61301.

ENERGY INFORMATION

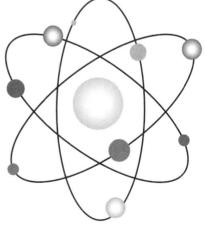

Everyone must do their share to save energy. The Conservation & Renewable Energy Inquiry & Referral Service (CAREIRS) has a nice information package any youngster would love to have: Learn what you can do to conserve energy. Excellent! Free from:
CAREIRS
PO Box 3048
Merrifield, VA 22116.

MICHAEL RECYCLE"

Here's a great comic for kids (& adults too) called *"Michael Recycle"*. Learn how you can recycle aluminum by collecting used aluminum products like soda cans and selling them back to the Reynolds Company to raise money for your

group while you do something good for the environment. For your free copy send a card to:
"MICHAEL RECYCLE", REYNOLDS ALUMINUM CO.
BOX 27003
RICHMOND, VA 23261
OR CALL TOLL-FREE: 1-800-228-2525

FUN-FILLED CATALOG
If you'd like a copy of what is probably the most unusual and funfilled catalog in the world, send for the *Johnson Smith Catalog*. It is filled with 1600 novelties, gadgets and fun-makers of every type. Send a postcard to:
JOHNSON SMITH CO.,
4514 19TH COURT E.
BRADENTON, FL 34203

DON'T GET HOOKED
The Office on Smoking and Health has a variety of colorful posters and interesting material explaining the real dangers of smoking. Ask for their free catalog of informative materials on smoking and your health. After you receive the catalog you can request the specific free materials you want. Send a postcard to:
OFFICE ON SMOKING AND HEALTH
PARK BLDG., 1-58
ROCKVILLE, MD 20857

TAKE A BITE OUT OF CRIME
The crime detective dog, McGruff will show you what you can do to fight crime. McGruff and his nephew, Scruff will send you a fun comic/ activity book that will show your children how to make themselves and their friends safer. They also have a *Parent's Streetwise Kids Guide.* Ask for *Scruff McGruff Take a Bite Out of Crime.* Call toll-free: **1-800-627-2911**
Or write to:
NATIONAL CRIME PREVENTION COUNCIL
1700 K STREET N.W. 2ND FLOOR
WASHINGTON, D.C. 20006-3817

Also, for a free action kit packed with ideas and real life experiences of what neighbors working together can do to prevent crime and make you and your family safer, call:
1-800-WE-PREVENT

Religion

CATHOLIC INFORMATION

The Knights of Columbus has dozens of booklets available on all aspects of the Catholic religion. The only cost is a nominal postage charge (generally 25¢ per booklet). They also have a 10 part home-study Catholic correspondence course that is free for the asking. The course is for both Catholics and non-Catholics who would like to learn more about Catholicism. It is sent in an unmarked envelope. For a complete *listing of publications* or to get your free correspondence course write to:

CATHOLIC INFORMATION SERVICE
KNIGHTS OF COLUMBUS
BOX 1971
NEW HAVEN, CT 06521

DAILY INSPIRATION

Our Daily Bread" provides inspirational readings from the scriptures for each day of the month. You'll get a new book each month. Ask them to add your name to their mailing list for this devotional guide plus discovery series booklets as well as a campus journal for young people. All free from:

RADIO BIBLE CLASS
P.O. BOX 2222
GRAND RAPIDS, MI 49555

NEWS NOTES

These *News Notes* are published by the Christophers 10 times a year and are free for the asking. The Christophers exist for one purpose: to spread the message that one person can make a difference in this world. Write and ask for information on titles available in any of these categories, News Note, books, videocassettes, they even have Spanish language issues. Drop a postcard to :

THE CHRISTOPHERS
12 EAST 48TH ST.
NEW YORK, NY 10017

INSPIRATION AND PRAYER

The Lutheran Laymen's League has several religious publications you might like to have. A few of the titles currently available are: *"Escape From Loneliness," "I Am An Alcoholic," "Stress - Problem or Opportunity?"* and *"The Truth About Angels."* All free from:
INTERNATIONAL LUTHERAN LAYMEN'S LEAGUE
2185 HAMPTON AVE.
ST. LOUIS, MO 63139

FREE FROM THE WORLDWIDE CHURCH OF GOD

The Worldwide Church of God has an excellent series of booklets available without charge (nor will they make any solicitations of any kind). Titles change frequently so drop a card for a current list of books available. Write to:
WORLDWIDE CHURCH OF GOD
PASADENA, CA 91123
OR CALL TOLL-FREE: **1-800-423-4444**

BEAUTIFUL INSPIRATION

Often in our daily lives events become too much to handle. The Salesian Missions have a beautiful series of booklets that are a pleasure to read and provide inspiration to help make our lives more fulfilling. Excellent! Drop a card for the *free inspirational booklets* from:
SALESIAN MISSIONS
2 LEFEVRES LANE
NEW ROCHELLE, NY 10801

GOSPEL OF JOHN COURSE

If you would like to learn more about the life of Christ, you can receive a free Gospel of John in English or Spanish (please specify) and a *Gospel of John Correspondence Course*. Drop a postcard to:
THE POCKET TESTAMENT LEAGUE
PO BOX 800
LITITZ, PA 17543

Special Free Offers

We've made special arrangements for readers of *The Best Free Things In America* to get a free watch or free credit card calculator (batteries *are* included) or both!

This beautiful 5-function Quartz Sport watch with World Time ($21.50 value) has an easy-to-read display that shows the hour, minutes, seconds, month and date and has a comfortable band.

Everyone can use an extra calculator. This full function Pocket Calculator ($8.95 value) is perfect for yourself or as a gift (or stocking stuffer). And best of all, it is free.

Please include $2.00 for shipping and handling for each watch or calculator you want. There is a limit of 5 watches and 5 calculators per person.

Just send your name & address and specify '*FREE WATCH*' or '*FREE CALCULATOR*'. Include $2.00 s&h for each item you want. Mail your request to:

DOLLAR STRETCHER
BFT-SPECIAL FREE OFFER
PO BOX 125
HARTSDALE, NY 10530

Learning Can Be Fun

"BASIC FACTS ABOUT THE UNITED NATIONS"

The organization, structure and all the agencies of the United Nations are a part of this fact filled book. You'll learn about the United Nations, all its members and how they work together to promote international peace and security. This book is absolutely free. Great for a school project. Ask for *"Basic Facts About the United Nations."* Drop a post card to:

UNITED NATIONS INFORMATION CENTRE
1889 "F" STREET NW
WASHINGTON, DC 20006

SKY GAZERS

If you enjoy studying the heavens, you will want to get a copy of Essential Magazines of Astronomy with a catalog of some of the finest astronomy books that will delight all star gazers. Write to:

SKY PUBLISHING CORP.
49 BAY STREET RD.
CAMBRIDGE, MA 02138

QUARTER HORSES

Whether you are presently an owner of horses or perhaps thinking of buying one - check out American Quarter Horses, the world's most popular breed of horse. Here's an interesting booklet you will want to have: *"For An American Quarter Horse."* For a copy of this fascinating booklet (and a colorful bumper sticker too), drop a card to:

AMERICAN QUARTER HORSE ASSN.
AMARILLO, TX 79168

TENNESSEE WALKING HORSE

Here's one every equestrian will want to have. Send a card for the 'Tennessee Walking Horse'

plus a colorful postcard showing the three horses chosen by the breeder's association as the world's greatest pleasure and show horse. Write to:

TENNESSEE WALKING HORSE
BOX 286
LEWISBURG, TN 37081

THOUGHTS TO PONDER

United Technologies has prepared an excellent series of thought provoking messages you will want to have. These inspirational messages come to you in a size suitable for framing. Write to:

DANIEL ISPONE, CHAIRMAN
UNITED TECHNOLOGIES
BOX 360
HARTFORD, CT 06141

SELF IMPROVEMENT

Would you like to take charge of your life — control your smoking, lose weight, attract more love or make more money? Maybe you should look through the *Love Tapes catalog*. Based on sound psychological principles, these tapes will help you develop your full potential. Send a card to:

EFFECTIVE LEARNING SYSTEMS
5221 EDINA IND. BLVD.
EDINA, MN 55435

"HOME FIRE DETECTION"

Learn how to protect your family and your home with smoke detectors—a must for all homes. Send a card to:

"HOME FIRE DETECTION,"
NATIONAL FIRE PROTECTION ASSOCIATION
BATTERYMARCH PARK
QUINCY, MA 02269

LOOK TO THE HEAVENS

Man has always been fascinated by the sky at night. With the recent discovery of planets circling around distant stars, one can't help but wonder whether life exists elsewhere in the universe. To find out more about our distant neighbors, send for the *skywatching series of booklets* dealing with our solar system and beyond. Send your request to:

PUBLIC AFFAIRS OFFICE
HARVARD SMITHSONIAN CENTER FOR ASTROPHYSICS
60 GARDEN ST.
CAMBRIDGE, MA 02138

ALL ABOUT COAL

A great information package-'*Coal Facts*'-tells the story of coal from A to Z. It contains many useful and instructive books, posters and even a helpful guide & samples of different types of coal teachers will love. To learn more about this important source of energy write to:

NATIONAL COAL FOUNDATION
1130 17TH ST. N.W. SUITE 2200
WASHINGTON, DC 20036

A SHARE OF AMERICA

"Getting Help When You Invest" and *"Understanding Stocks and Bonds"* and two fascinating guides that tells all about how the stock market works and the important role it plays in our nation's economy. The New York Stock Exchange also has an excellent series of educational aids, huge wall posters, ticker tape, teacher guides and more. Incidentally teachers can get a package tailored to the grade level they're teaching. Quantities of books will be supplied for each student. Write to:

N.Y. STOCK EXCHANGE
EDUCATIONAL SERVICES
11 WALL ST.
NEW YORK, NY 10005

THE WRIGHT BROTHERS

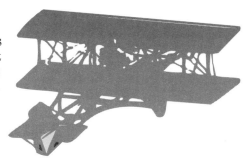

With men on the moon and rockets to Jupiter it's hard to believe that manned flight began just 87 years ago with an historic 120 foot journey that lasted all of 12 seconds. All the fascinating details are found in this historical recap, *"Wright Brothers'*. Send a card to:

WRIGHT BROTHERS NATIONAL MEMORIAL

ROUTE 1, BOX 676
MANTEO, NC 27954

CONSUMERS AGAINST GOVERNMENT WASTE

If you would like to find out what the massive federal deficit actually means to you and your children, get a copy of the free booklet by calling this toll-free number: **1-800-USA-DEBT**

TRUTH ABOUT NUCLEAR ENERGY

Is nuclear energy the answer to our energy needs or are the risks of nuclear disaster just too great? To help you answer this question, here is an excellent package of books that is free for the asking. Topics covered include nuclear power plants, the structure of the atom, magnetic fusion, the story of nuclear energy and a whole lot more. They will also include information about wind energy and conservation. Ask for the *"Nuclear Energy information package.* Very informative. All free from:
U.S. DEPARTMENT OF ENERGY
PO BOX 62
OAK RIDGE, TN 37830

AUSTRALIA TODAY

What is life like 'down-under'? *"Australia Now"* will give you a look—in full color-at what's happening in Australia today. You'll also receive vacation planning, travel tips and information on locations, tours and accommodations. Drop a postcard to:
AUSTRALIAN CONSULATE GENERAL
630 FIFTH AVE. SUITE 420
NEW YORK NY 10111

PHOTO TIME

Want some photo tips from the experts? The folks at Kodak have a fascinating booklet you will want to get, "Self-Teaching Guide To Picture Taking." If you take black and white pictures and want to know the best film speed for you or the best flash exposure, you'll definitely want a copy of *"Kodak Black and White Films*

For General Picture Taking." Send a card to:
EASTMAN KODAK
343 STATE STREET
ROCHESTER, NY 14650

"STORY OF COTTON"

Here's a huge wall poster with colorful illustrations showing the development of cotton
from seed to clothing. Also included will be an
interesting book on cotton. The kids will love
this. All free from:
NATIONAL COTTON COUNCIL
PO BOX 12285
MEMPHIS, TN 38112

FACTS ABOUT OIL

This nicely illustrated guide to petroleum tells
all about the history of oil exploration and shows
how the search for oil is conducted. Ask for the
"energy information series" and you'll receive a
great package of excellent booklets dealing with
many forms of energy including wind, nuclear,
geothermal, coal, oil and more. Send a card to:
AMERICAN PETROLEUM INSTITUTE
PUBLICATIONS SECTION 1220 L ST. N.W.
WASHINGTON, DC 20005

THE REAL DEAL

Everyone spends money, but not everyone
knows how to do it right. Spending money
wisely takes skill, time and experience. To help
you learn how to shop smart, the FTC and the
National Association of Attorneys General have
put together a fun activity booklet called "The
Real Deal." To get your free copy, write to:
YOUR STATE ATTORNEY GENERAL
OFFICE OF CONSUMER PROTECTION
YOUR STATE CAPITAL
OR TO: THE FEDERAL TRADE COMMISSION
6TH & PENNSYLVANIA AVE., NW ROOM 403
WASHINGTON, DC 20580
WORLD WIDE WEB SITE AT: HTTP://WWW.FTC.GOV

ALUMINUM CARS?

Today, through greater use of aluminum parts

our cars are getting far better miles per gallon. This is just one of the many uses of aluminum. If you would like a better understanding of the history of aluminum, the ways it is made and how it's used, ask for the free *"Story of Aluminum* and *"Alcoa"* from:

ALCOA
150 ALCOA BUILDING.
PITTSBURGH, PA 15219

FORD GRANTS

Since 1936 the Ford Foundation has committed close to $6 billion to 7900 institutions and organizations in the U.S. and 96 foreign countries. *"Ford Foundation Current Interests"* tells all about the great philanthropic work they sponsor. Write to:

FORD FOUNDATION
320 43RD ST.
NEW YORK, NY 10017

CLEAN ENVIRONMENT

Bethlehem Steel would like you to know what they are doing to clean up the air and water. For example, at one plant they have spent over 100 million dollars for air and water quality controls. For a free copy of *"Steelmaking & The Environment,"* send a card to:

BETHLEHEM STEEL CORP.
PUBLIC AFFAIRS DEPT., ROOM 476MT
BETHLEHEM, PA 18016

BE A BETTER WRITER

The National Council of Teachers of English have compiled some handy tips to help make your children better writers. If they start with good writing skills as early as possible, they will have no problem with the written word later on. Ask for *"How to Help Your Child Become A Better Writer."* Specify English or Spanish edition. Send a SASE to:

NATIONAL COUNCIL OF TEACHERS OF ENGLISH
DEPT. C, 1111 KENYON RD.
URBANA, IL 61801

CHAMBER OF COMMERCE

What Is the Chamber of Commerce? Who runs it? What does it do? For a concise booklet answering your questions, write to:

CHAMBER OF COMMERCE OF THE **U.S.**
1615 H ST. N.W.
WASHINGTON, DC 20062

PITCH THIS ONE!

If you have ever thought about taking up horse shoe pitching, now's the time. (Did you know that former President George Bush used to pitch horseshoes?) To find out more about this fun sport and to learn all the rules and tips for throwing the perfect horseshoe pitch. Send for your free copy of the *Official Rules For Horseshoe Pitching*. Send a SASE to:

NHPA, RR2
BOX 178
LAMONTE, MD 65337

MAZES

If you like puzzles and mazes, you will love this freebie. You will receive a complimentary maze valued at $3.95. Write and ask for it from:

PDK ENTERPRISES
PO BOX 1776
BOYES HOT SPRINGS, CA 95416

FREE SAMPLE SCIENCE PROJECT PLAN

If you like to do science experiments, this one's for you. You'll receive a science project plan which lists materials needed and gives instruction about how to do the project. Includes a full listing of 265 others available at nominal cost. Great for science students and teachers. Send a name & address label and 2 first class postage stamps to:

THE MAD SCIENTIST
PO BOX 50182
KNOXVILLE, TN 37950

College & Beyond

FREE COLLEGE AID

There are literally billions of millions of dollars in financial aid available to help students pay for their college education. This money is available from thousands of public and private sources. Much of this money is available as outright grants that never has to be repaid. Still more money for college is available through low-cost loans and work-study programs. The first place to check is with the financial aid office of the college of your choice. Counselors will help you locate all the sources of money including scholarships, grant-in-aid, work study programs and low interest government-backed student loans. Other sources of assistance are listed below.

MONEY FOR COLLEGE

Sallie Mae is the leading source of money for college loans. They can help you with the two extremely important things: guidance and savings. When you call, they will give you information about paying for college, loans, aid packages, deadlines, and lots more. You will also learn how to save hundreds with the lowest cost student loans available. Loans with Sallie Mae can cost a lot less to pay back. Call Sallie Mae at:
1-800-806-3681

STUDENT LOANS

If you're a student short of money to continue

your education, a *free booklet* of available federal financial aid programs can be obtained from:
THE U.S. DEPARTMENT OF EDUCATION,
400 MARYLAND AVE. S.W. ROOM 2097
WASHINGTON. D.C. 20202

COLLEGE PLANNING

T. Rowe Price's College Planning Guide helps parents project what a college education may cost for their young children. It's absolutely free. Call: (1-800-225-5132)

FINANCIAL AID

"Financial Aid from the U.S. Department of Education: Grants, Loans and Work-Study." Student guide to obtaining federal money lists sources, guidelines for eligibility, application procedures, deadlines, phone numbers, and more. It's free from:
CONSUMER INFORMATION CENTER
DEPT 506X
PUEBLO, CO 81009

PAYING FOR COLLEGE

With the cost of going to college skyrocketing every year, you may be wondering how to pay for your education. "Meeting College Costs" will help you with all the questions you have about paying for your college education. Ask for *"Meeting College Costs"* free from:
THE COLLEGE BOARD
45 COLUMBUS AVE.
NEW YORK, NY 10023-6992

COMPARING COLLEGE COSTS

Computer users can quickly compare the cost of more than 1500 public and private colleges and get an estimate of what it will cost to attend. When you call, ask for *"College Savings Plus,"* a free computer disk available from John Hancock Mutual Life Insurance Co. After you ask for the free computer disk, a John Hancock agent will likely call to ask if you want help

devising a savings plan. Call:
1-800-633-1809

WEAR GUARD

This is the catalog for you, if you are looking for sturdy work force clothes. These clothes are industrial strength -you'll find insulated overalls, heavy duty work pants, rain gear, even Timberland foot gear. Send a postcard to:

WEAR GUARD WORK CLOTHES
LONGWATER DRIVE
NORWELL, MA 02061
OR CALL **1-800-388-3300**

FOR A FREE FOOTWEAR CATALOG, WITH OVER 150 STYLES OF STEEL TOE, WORK BOOTS, DRESS SHOES, ATHLETIC SHOES, HIKERS, RUBBER BOOTS AND MORE, CALL **1-800-388-3300**

FOR A FREE CATALOG OF FLAME RESISTANT WORK CLOTHES,
CALL **1-800-950-8820**

PROFESSIONAL HEALTH CARE APPAREL, FEATURES FAMOUS CREST HEALTH CARE UNIFORMS OF ALL KINDS CALL **1-800-967-5829.**

WANT TO RENT UNIFORMS, CALL ARATEX:
800-327-2839

MEETING COLLEGE COSTS

With the costs of going to college spiraling out of sight many students are not able to attend college without financial assistance. This guide can help you learn whether you're eligible for student aid. Write to:

COLLEGE BOARD PUBLICATIONS
"BIBLIOGRAPHY OF FINANCIAL AID"
45 COLUMBUS AVE.
NEW YORK, NY 10023

JOB SEARCH

If you are thinking about or seriously looking for a job, this report on *"How to Have a Successful Job Search."* is a must for you. This valuable report will provide you with information critical to you and your job search. The author, Kay La Rocca is a professional resume writer and expert on what's out there. Ask for *"How*

to Have A Successful Job Search." Send a long SASE to:
KL PUBLICATIONS
4003 FOREST DR.
ALQUIPPA, PA 15001

FINDING THE RIGHT JOB

If you're confused about what career direction to go in, get a copy of *"Tips For Finding The Right Job."* It will help you evaluate your interests and skills. Write:
EMPLOYMENT & TRAINING
USDL, 200 CONSTITUTION AVE NW, ROOM N4700
WASHINGTON, DC 20210

WORK ABROAD!

If you ever wanted to work in a London Pub, or at an office complex or any where in Great Britain this is your chance. As a student you are afforded the once in a lifetime chance to legally work in another country. For information on how to work in Great Britain or other countries, write or call.
WORK ABROAD
CIEE 305 E. 42 ST.
NEW YORK, NY 10017
1-212-661-1414 EXT. 1126

Looking Good

PANTYHOSE

The National Association of Hosiery Manufacturers would like to help you overcome your fear of stocking runs, snags and droops. They will provide you with valuable information and helpful tips on how to determine your correct size, stocking care and how to make your hosiery last. Call them with any specific questions you may have about stockings. Call:
1-800-346-7379

LEG TALK

Has this ever happened to you: you're down to your last pair of stockings and late for an important meeting when, for no apparent reason, the stockings 'run'? Would you like to find out why this happens and what you can do about it? Write for your free copy of *"Sheer Facts About Hosiery.*

NATIONAL HOSIERY ASSN.
200 N. SHARON AMITY BLVD.
CHARLOTTE, NC 28211

WARDROBE PLANNING GUIDE FOR WOMEN

How should you dress for work? When is casual attire appropriate and when is it not? The Lee Company has a free wardrobe guide that will help you answer these questions. The guide presents 10 clothing selections that you can mix and match to wear anywhere. It will not only help you put together a basic wardrobe, but will also recommend accessories that will take your daytime into evening and weekday into weekend wear. A must for every woman. To get your free copy of *Ten Easy Pieces,* call:
1-800-4-LEE-FIT

ASK THE HAIR COLORING EXPERTS

Are you thinking of changing your hair color?

Having trouble finding the right shade? Can't cover that problem gray? The experts at Clairol have a toll-free hotline you can call for answers to all your hair coloring questions. Their color consultants will also provide you with helpful tips that will help you look your very best. Call them Monday-Friday 8:30am-8:30pm or Saturday 9am-6pm EST at: **1-800-233-5800.**
You can also visit the Clairol Women's Link site on the Internet at: www.womenslink.com

HAIR CARE GUIDANCE & MORE

If you would like advice on how to manage your hair, how to color it or just how to keep it looking good, L'Oreal has the answers for you. Next time you can't decide which shampoo or conditioner is best for your hair type, call the toll-free L'Oreal Guideline Monday-Friday, 10am-7pm EST at:
1-800-631-7358 or you can write to them at:
L'OREAL CONSUMER AFFAIRS
PO BOX 98
WESTFIELD, NJ 07091

BEAUTY IS SKIN DEEP

Has anyone ever told you, "you are what you eat." The basics of looking good and feeling good, start with healthy eating habits. The American Dietetic Association is making a concerted effort to get us back on a healthy eating track. They have a toll-free phone line you can call weekdays for more information on healthy eating and a referral service to local dietician. Call the Consumer Nutrition HotLine at:
1-800-366-1655

KEEP IT CLEAN

The makers of Moisturel Products would like to show you just how good their skin cleansers and lotions are. If you drop them a card they will send you a *$1.00 discount coupon* good on your next purchase of Moisturel products. Send a card to:
WESTWOOD PHARMACEUTICALS
468 DEWITT ST.
BUFFALO, NY 14213

Computers

PC & MAC CONNECTION
If you are looking for the best deals around in computers, software and accessories some of the best prices you will find are from mail order companies. Even if you decide to buy from a local store, calling mail order companies will allow you to comparison shop to get the lowest price. Each of the companies listed here have been in business for a number of years and have an excellent reputation for customer satisfaction. When you call ask for their latest catalog which will be full of important information to all you to make an intelligent buying decision. Most have a 24 hour customer service line and your orders arrive promptly, often the very next day
PC Connection: **1-800-800-1111**
Mac Connection: **1-800-800-0002**
PC Warehouse & MacWarehouse:
1-800 255-6227
Micro Warehouse: **1-800-367-7080**
CD ROM Warehouse: **1-800-237-6623**
DataCOM: **1-800-328-2261**
DirectWare: **1-800 490-9273**
MacZONE: **1-800-248-0800**
PC ZONE: **1-800-258-2088**
Tiger: **1-800-888-4437**
MacMALL: **1-800-222-2808**
Educorp: **1-800-843-9497**
MEI: **1-800-634-3478**

APPLE ASSISTANCE
If you own a Macintosh or are thinking of buying one and have questions you need answered, there's a toll-free number you can call for help.
Apple Help line: **1-800-SOS-APPL**

FREE COMPUTER BUSINESS INFORMATION
Computer Business Services will send you free cassettes and color literature on one of today's quickest growing industries. We all know the computer industry has taken off like a rocket,

and now it's possible for you to be a part of it. To receive free cassettes and color literature on their business opportunities, call **1-800-343-8014**, or write to:
COMPUTER BUSINESS SERVICES
CBSI PLAYA, STE. 1180
SHERIDAN, IN 46069

COMPUTER SUPPLY CATALOG

If you or your company owns a computer you will want to get a copy of the *Inmac Computer Supplies Catalog*. This full color catalog lists more than 2,000 PC & Macintosh computer-related products of all types, drop a postcard to:
INMAC
2300 VALLEY VIEW LAND, SUITE 200
IRVING, TX 75062
OR CALL: 1-800-547-5444

THE WORLD AT YOUR FINGER TIP

One of the major advantages of owning a personal computer is that you can stay in touch with people and sources of information that may be thousands of miles from you. In an instant you can surf the Internet, get a stock quote, read the Associated Press News hot off the wire, play an adventure game with someone across the country, shop at home, and hundreds of other information services. For more information, write for *"Compuserve's How To Get Started Package"* including free hours from:
Compuserve
5000 Arlington Centre Blvd.
Columbus, OH 43220.
Or call toll-free: **1-800-848-8199**

FREE SOFTWARE STUDENT SPECIAL

Professor Weissman will send you a free educational computer disc for PC's and compatibles. He has great programs including algebra, trigonometry, precalculus, statistics and math for nursing. All you have to do is include $2.00 postage & handling (or a SASE requesting more information) to:

PROFESSOR WEISSMAN'S SOFTWARE
246 CRAFTON AVE.
STATEN ISLAND, NY 10314

FREE ON THE INTERNET

Thousands of pieces of software are available absolutely free on the Internet. If you have a computer and a modem, accessing the Internet is a simple and easy way to open up a whole new world. Among other things, you will find 'freeware', 'shareware' and free computer application upgrades waiting for you to download into your computer. You will also find full text of hundreds of useful government booklets and reports on a host of fascinating subjects all of which you can download free.

FREE COMPUTER SUPPLIES

Right now there's intense competition going on between several nationwide computer retailers. To bring you into their store, each of them offers free computer supplies with a full rebate. For example in the last several weeks we have received several hundred computer diskettes, surge protectors, laser paper, a computer mouse, and other computer related items all of which came with a 100% rebate. Hundreds of dollars in supplies absolutely free! Check your local newspaers for full page ads and inserts for CompUSA, Computer City, Circuit City and other chain stores.

Conservation

INVITE BIRDS OVER

This large colorful poster-like guide will show you how to *"Invite Birds To Your Home."* It tells how to attract birds with proper tree plantings that specific species prefer. You also might want to ask for *"Your Hometown, Clean Water Town"*. For your free copy write:

SOIL CONSERVATION SERVICE
U.S.D.A.
BOX 2890
WASHINGTON, DC 20013

FOREST CONSERVATION

The book you're reading right now and the lumber in the house in which you live are just two of the many products we take for granted that come from our nation's forests. It is essential that we take care to preserve and renew our forests. The U.S. Forest Service has a booklet you will want to have: *"Making Paper From Trees"* shows how a tree goes from the forest and ends up as paper. Send a postcard to:

FOREST SERVICE
U.S. DEPT. OF AGRICULTURE
BOX 2417
WASHINGTON, DC 20013

TROUT RESTOCKING AID

If you would like to restock your lake or pond, contact the Federal Hatcheries first. They offer free assistance in your restocking plans. If their production is sufficient, they may be able to supply the trout you need. They also have an interesting booklet you might want, *"Endangered & Threatened Wildlife and Plants."* Write to:

U.S. DEPARTMENT OF THE INTERIOR
FISH & WILDLIFE SERVICE
WASHINGTON, DC 20240

For Sports Fans

Do you love sports? How would you like to receive photos of your favorite teams? Most sports clubs have all kinds of freebies for their loyal fans. These neat freebies often include team photos, souvenir brochures, stickers, fan club information, playing schedules, catalogs and lots more. All you have to do is write to your favorite sports teams at the addresses in this book. Tell them you're a loyal fan and ask them for a "fan package."

Even though it's not always necessary, it's always nice idea to send a long self-addressed-stamped envelope with your name & address written in so they can return your freebie right in your own envelope.

Also, if you have a favorite player on the team, write his name on the envelope.

Sometimes it takes a while to get an answer since most teams are absolutely flooded with mail. Just be patient and you will hear from them.

HOCKEY

NATIONAL HOCKEY LEAGUE
75 INTERNATIONAL BLVD. SUITE 300
REXDALE, ONTARIO CANADA M9W 6L9

EASTERN CONFERENCE

Boston Bruins
1 Fleet Center, Suite 250
Boston, MA 02114

Buffalo Sabres
Memorial Auditorium
140 Main St
Buffalo, NY 14202

Florida Panthers
Miami Arena
100 NE Third Ave., 10th Fl
Ft. Lauderdale, FL 33301

Hartford Whalers
Civic Center
242 Trumbell Dr.
Hartford, CT 06013

Montreal Canadians
2313 St. Catherine St. West
Montreal, Quebec, Canada H3H 1N2

New Jersey Devils
Byrne Meadowlands
Arena
PO Box 504
E. Rutherford, NJ 07073

New York Islanders
Nassau Coliseum
Uniondale, NY 11553

New York Rangers
Madison Square Garden
4 Penn Plaza
New York, NY 10001

Ottawa Senators
301 Moodie Dr., Suite 200
Nepean, Ontario,
Canada K2H 9C4

Philadelphia Flyers
The Spectrum
Pattison Place
Philadelphia, PA 19148

Pittsburgh Penguins
Civic Arena, Gate No. 9
Pittsburgh, PA 15219

Tampa Bay Lightning
501 E. Kennedy Blvd.,
Suite 175
Tampa, FL 33602

Washington Capitals
U.S. Air Arena
Landover, MD 20785

WESTERN CONFERENCE

Anaheim Mighty Ducks
Arrowhead Pond of
Anaheim
2695 Katella Ave
Anaheim, CA 92806

Calgary Flames
Olympic Saddledome
PO Box 1540, Station M
Calgary, Alberta,
Canada T2P 3B9

Chicago Blackhawks
1901 W. Madison
Chicago, IL 60612

Colorado Avalanche
1635 Clay St.
Denver, CO 80204

Dallas Stars
211 Cowboys Pkwy
Irving, TX 75063

Detroit Red Wings
Joe Louis Arena
600 Civic Center Dr.
Detroit, MI 48226

Edmonton Oilers
Northland Coliseum
7424-118 Ave
Edmonton, Alberta,

Canada T5B 4M9

Los Angeles Kings
PO Box 17013
Inglewood, CA 90308

St. Louis Blues
PO Box 66792
St. Louis, MO 63166-6792

St. Jose Sharks
St. Jose Arena
525 W. Santa Clara St.
San Jose, CA 95113

Toronto Maple Leafs
Maple Leaf Gardens
60 Carlton St
Toronto, Ontario,
Canada M5B 1L1

Vancouver Canucks
Pacific Coliseum
100 N. Renfrew St
Vancouver, B.C.,
Canada V5K 3N7

Winnipeg Jets
10th Fl., 1661 Portage Ave.
Winnipeg, Manitoba,
Canada R3J 3T7

NATIONAL BASKETBALL ASSOCIATION

Atlanta Hawks
1 CNN Center
South Tower, Suite 405
Atlanta, GA 30303

Boston Celtics
151 Merrimac St., 4th Fl.
Boston, MA 02114

Charlotte Hornets Fan Mail
100 Hive Dr.
Charlotte, NC 28217

Chicago Bulls
1901 West Madison
Chicago, IL 6O612-4501

Cleveland Cavaliers
1 Center Court
Cleveland, OH 44115

Dallas Mavericks
Reunion Arena
777 Sports St.
Dallas, TX 75207

Denver Nuggets
1635 Clay St.
Denver, CO 80204

Detroit Pistons
2 Championship Dr.
Auburn Hills, MI 48326

Golden State Warriors
Oakland Coliseum Arena
7000 Coliseum Way
Oakland, CA 94621

Houston Rockets
10 Greenway Plaza
Houston, TX 77046

Indiana Pacers
300 E. Market St.
Indianapolis, IN 46204

Los Angeles Clippers
L.A. Memorial Sports
Arena
3939 S. Figueroa
Los Angeles, CA 90037

Los Angeles Lakers
Great Western Forum
P.O. Box 10
Inglewood, CA 90306

Miami Heat
1 Southeast Third Ave.
Miami, FL 33131

Milwaukee Bucks
1001 N. 4th St.
Milwaukee, WI 53203

Minnesota Timberwolves
600 1st Ave. North
Minneapolis, MN 55403

New Jersey Nets
405 Murray Hill Parkway
E. Rutherford, NJ 07073

New York Knicks
Madison Square Garden
2 Penn Plaza
New York, NY 10121

Orlando Magic
P.O. Box 76
Orlando, FL 32802

Philadelphia '76ers
Veteran Stadium
P.O. Box 25040
Philadelphia, PA 19147

Phoenix Suns
P.O. Box 1369
Phoenix, AZ 85001

Portland Trail Blazers
700 N.E. Multnomah St.
Ste 600
Portland, OR 97232

Sacramento Kings
1 Sports Parkway
Sacramento, CA 95834

San Antonio Spurs
100 Montana Street
San Antonio, TX 78203

Seattle Supersonics
P.O. Box C900911
Seattle, WA 98109-9711

Toronto Raptors
20 Bay Street Ste. 702
Toronto, Ontario
Canada M5J 2N8

Utah Jazz
301 W. South Temple
Salt Lake City, UT 84101

Vancouver Grizzlies
General Motors Place
800 Griffith Way
Vancouver, BC
Canada V6B 6G1

Washington Bullets
U.S. Air Arena
Landover, MD 20785

• • • • • • • • • • • • • •

FOOTBALL

NATIONAL FOOTBALL LEAGUE
410 PARK AVE.
NEW YORK, NY 10022

AMERICAN CONFERENCE FOOTBALL TEAMS

Baltimore Ravens
11001 Owings Mills Blvd.
Owings Mills, MD 21117

Buffalo Bills
1 Bills Dr.
Orchard Park, NY 14127

Cincinnati Bengals
200 Riverfront Stadium
Cincinnati, OH 45202

Denver Broncos
13655 Broncos Pkwy.
Englewood, CO 80112

Houston Oilers
6910 Fannin St.
Houston, TX 77030

Indianapolis Colts
7001 W. 56th St.
Indianapolis, IN 46253

Jacksonville Jaguars
One Stadium Place
Jacksonville, FL 32202

Kansas City Chiefs
1 Arrowhead Dr.
Kansas City, MO 64129

Miami Dolphins
Joe Robbie Stadium
2269 NW 199th St.
Miami, FL 33056

New England Patriots
Foxboro Stadium -
Route 1
Foxboro, MA 02035

New York Jets
1000 Fulton Ave.
Hempstead, NY 11550

Oakland Raiders
332 Center St
El Segundo, CA 90245

Pittsburgh Steelers
Three Rivers Stadium
300 Stadium Cir.
Pittsburgh, PA 15212

San Diego Chargers
P.O. Box 609609
San Diego, CA 92160

Seattle Seahawks
11220 NE 53rd St.
Kirkland, WA 98033

NATIONAL CONFERENCE FOOTBALL TEAMS

Arizona Cardinals
PO Box 888
Tempe, AZ 85001

Atlanta Falcons
2745 Burnette Road
Suwanee,GA 30174

Carolina Panthers
227 W. Trade St., Suite 1600
Charlotte, NC 28202

Chicago Bears
Halas Hall
250 N. Washington Rd.
Lake Forest, IL 60045

Dallas Cowboys
Cowboys Center
1 Cowboys Pkwy.
Irving, TX 75063

Detroit Lions
1200 Featherstone Rd.
Pontiac, MI 48342

Green Bay Packers
1265 Lombardi Ave.
Green Bay, WI 54304

Minnesota Vikings
9520 Viking Dr.
Eden Prairie, MN 55344

New Orleans Saints
5800 Airline Hwy
Metairie, LA 70003

New York Giants
Giants Stadium
East Rutherford, NJ 07073

Philadelphia Eagles
Broad Street & Pattison Ave.
Philadelphia, PA 19148

San Francisco 49ers
4949 Centennial Blvd.
Santa Clara, CA 95054

St. Louis Rams
100 North Broadway, Ste. 2100
St. Louis, MO 63102

Tampa Bay Buccaneers
1 Buccaneer Pl.
Tampa, FL 33607

Washington Redskins
PO Box 17247
Dallas International Airport
Washington, D.C. 20041

BASEBALL

MAJOR LEAGUE BASEBALL
350 PARK AVE.
NEW YORK, NY 10022

AMERICAN LEAGUE
BASEBALL TEAMS

Baltimore Orioles
333 W. Camden Street
Baltimore, MD 21201

Boston Red Sox
Fenway Park
Boston, MA 02115

California Angels
P.O. Box 2000
Anaheim, CA 92803

Chicago White Sox
333 W. 35th St.
Chicago, IL 60616

Cleveland Indians
Jacobs Field
2401 Ontario Street
Cleveland, OH 44115

Detroit Tigers
Public Relations
2121 Trumbull Ave.
Detroit, MI 48216

Kansas City Royals
P.O. Box 419969
Kansas City, MO 64141

Milwaukee Brewers
P.O. Box 3099
Milwaukee, WI 53201

Minnesota Twins
501 Chicago Ave. South
Minneapolis, MN 55415

New York Yankees
Yankee Stadium
Bronx, NY 10451

Oakland Athletics
Oakland Coliseum
Oakland, CA 94621

Seattle Mariners
P.O. Box 4100
Seattle, WA 98104

Texas Rangers
P.O. Box 90111
Arlington, TX 76004

Toronto Blue Jays
1 Blue Jay Way
Sky Dome
300 Bremmer Blvd.,
Suite 3200
Toronto, Ont.,
Canada MSV 3B3

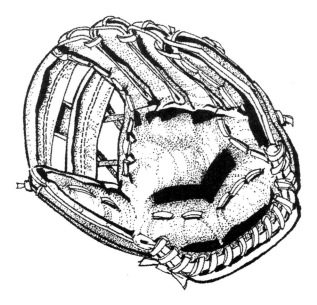

NATIONAL LEAGUE
BASEBALL TEAMS

Atlanta Braves
P.O. Box 4064
Atlanta, GA 30302

Chicago Cubs
Wrigley Field
1060 West Addison St.
Chicago, IL 60613

Cincinnati Reds
100 Riverfront Stadium
Cincinnati, OH 45202

Colorado Rockies
1700 Broadway Ste 2100
Denver, CO 80205

Florida Marlins
Joe Robbie Stadium
2267 NW 199th St.
Miami, FL 33056

Houston Astros
P.O. Box 288
Houston, TX 77001-0288

Los Angeles Dodgers
1000 Elysian Park Ave.
Los Angeles, CA 90012

Montreal Expos
PO Box 500, Station M
Montreal, Quebec,
Canada HIV 3P2

New York Mets
Shea Stadium
Flushing, NY 11368

Philadelphia Phillies
Veteran Stadium
P.O. Box 7575
Philadelphia, PA 19101

Pittsburgh Pirates
Three Rivers Stadium
Pittsburgh, PA 15212

St. Louis Cardinals
250 Stadium Plaza
St. Louis, MO 63102

San Diego Padres
P.O. Box 2000
San Diego, CA 92112

San Francisco Giants
Candlestick Park
San Francisco, CA 94124

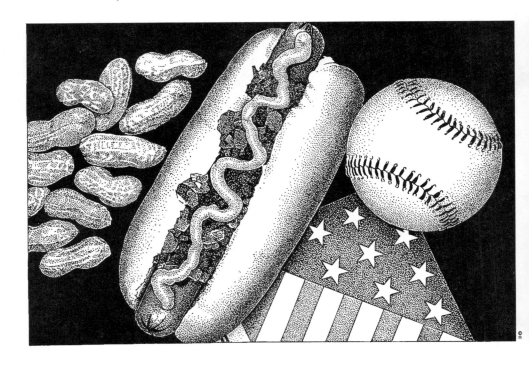

OUTDOOR SPORTS

L. L. Bean, the outdoor sporting specialists for 67 years, would like to send you a copy of their *catalog*. It features apparel and footwear for the outdoorsman or woman as well as equipment for camping, fishing, hiking and canoeing. Drop a card to:

L.L. BEAN
FREEPORT, ME 04033

PHYSICAL FITNESS

It's always a great idea to get in shape and stay in shape. This physical fitness package is full of all kinds of information that will help you take better care of your body. You'll get an introduction to exercise, weight control, physical fitness, sports, running and lots more. Drop a card to:

THE PRESIDENT'S COUNCIL ON PHYSICAL FITNESS & SPORTS
WASHINGTON, D.C. 20201.
LITTLE LEAGUE BASEBALL, INC.
P.O. BOX 3485
WILLIAMSPORT, PA 17701

THE OLYMPIC GAMES

"The History of The Olympics" gives you the complete story of the Olympics starting with the earliest recorded game in 776 B.C. and traces the games' history through the present. For your free copy write:

U.S. OLYMPIC COMMITTEE
1750 EAST BOULDER ST.
COLORADO SPRINGS, CO 80909

AMATEUR ATHLETICS

If you're involved with amateur sports in any way this is for you. *"The AAU Youth Sports Program"* is a big 66 page book covering 15 sports with official rules. Free from:

AAU ORDER DEPT.
3400 W. 86TH ST.
INDIANAPOLIS, IN 46268

LITTLE LEAGUE BASEBALL

Little League Baseball has built character, team play, physical fitness and most importantly—the drive to win—in thousands of youngsters throughout America. If you're involved (or plan to be involved) with the Little League you may want to get a copy of the *Little League Baseball Equipment Supplies catalog*. It's free from:

LITTLE LEAGUE BASEBALL, INC.
P.O. BOX 3485
WILLIAMSPORT, PA 17701

HOCKEY CARDS

If you are a hockey fan, you'll definitely want to send for this freebie. You will receive 10 free hockey cards. To get your cards, send a SASE and 50¢ to:

DANORS, DEPARTMENT H
5721 FUNSTON STREET BAY 14
HOLLYWOOD, FL 33023

Cars & Drivers

TIRES

Did you know that when you keep your tires properly inflated that the air provides a cushion of protection when you hit a pothole. If the tire is under inflated you could damage the wheel. If it is over inlated the tire will be damaged. For the best information around for caring and protecting your tires send for a free copy of *"The Motorist Tire Care and Safety Guide."* Send a SASE to:

TIRE INDUSTRY SAFETY COUNCIL
PO Box 3147
MEDINA, OHIO, 44258

CAR TROUBLE?

Call the National Highway Safety Auto Complaint line for any technical problems you are having with your vehicle that you feel might be the result of a manufacturing defect.
1-800-445-0197

BUY A CAR?
LEASE A CAR?

If you can't decide whether to buy or lease a vehicle you need to have this guide *"A Consumer Education Guide to Leasing vs. Buying"* from the National Vehicle Leasing Association, write your name and address on a 3 x 5 card and send it with $1.00 postage & handling to:

HEGGEN & ASSOCIATES INC.
PO Box 5025
EVANSTON, IL 60204-5025

"BE A GOOD NEIGHBOR, BE A DESIGNATED DRIVER"

State Farm wants to help give you, your college, civic group or professional organization free designated driver items. They're a colorful way to remind your friends and associates of the importance of safe driving. They will send your group a free designated driver kit. It has a presentation guide, video and sample speeches. Write to:

STATE FARM INSURANCE COMPANIES
ACTION NETWORK-PUBLIC AFFAIRS
DESIGNATED DRIVER PROGRAM
ONE STATE FARM PLAZA
BLOOMINGTON, IL 61710

A SAFER CAR

"Injury, Collision and Theft Losses - Shopping For A Safer Car" will help you make an intelligent choice of the safest vehicle for you. It provides you with an excellent safety and loss comparisons for hundreds of passenger cars, vans, pick ups and utility vehicle models. Write to:

HIGHWAY LOSS DATA INSTITUTE, DEPT R 92-2
1005 N. GLEBE RD., SUITE 800
ARLINGTON, VA 22201

LEARN ABOUT OIL

Quaker State Pocket Planner is an excellent guide that tells you how to read an oil can, what the SAE number means, which oil is best for you and lots more. Every motorist should read this guide. You'll also receive a free keychain and bumper sticker. Free from:

QUAKER STATE OIL
BOX 989
OIL CITY, PA 16301

FOR AAA MEMBERS

If you're a member of AAA they offer an excellent tour service. Tell them where you want to drive and they'll give you detailed road maps with your route outlined in pencil. Contact your local AAA office for this service.

HELP FOR CAR OWNERS

If you're having problems with your car and can't seem to get satisfaction from the manufacturer don't despair - help is on the way. The National Highway Traffic Safety Commission is anxious to hear about your complaint so they can get to work on it. They've even set up a toll-free hotline for you to call to report your problem. To report your problem, call toll-free: **1-800-424-9393. OR DROP A LINE TO:**
THE NATIONAL HIGHWAY SAFETY ADMINISTRATION
400 7TH ST., S.W.
WASHINGTON, **DC 20590**

AUTOMOBILE HOTLINE NUMBERS

If you plan to buy or lease a car in the near future, be sure you get all the information you need to make an intelligent decision. Call the toll-free hotline phone number of the cars you are interested in. They will send you beautiful color product information booklets

Acura	1-800-TO-ACURA
BMW	1-800-334-4BMW
Buick	1-800-4-RIVIERA
Cadillac	1-800-333-4CAD
Chevy Monte Carlo & Geo	1-800-950-2438
Chevy Tahoe	1-800-950-TAHOE
Chrysler	1-800-4-A-CHRYSLER
Dodge	1-800-4-A-DODGE
Eagle Vision Tsi	1-800-2-TEST-EAGLE
Ford	1-800-392-3673
GMC Sierra	1-800-GMC-TRUCK
Honda	1-800-33-HONDA Ext 435
Hyundai	1-800-826-CARS
Infiniti	1-800-950-8074
Isuzu	1-800-726-2700
Jaguar	1-800-4-JAGUAR

Jeep 1-800-925-JEEP

Land Rover 1-800-FINE-4WD

Lexus 1-800-USA-LEXUS

Lincoln 1-800-446-8888

Mercedes 1-800-FOR-MERCEDES

Mercury 1-800-531-6870

Mitsubishi 1-800-55-MITSU

Nissan.................................. 1-800-NISSAN-3

Oldsmobile 1-800-448-0092

Oldsmobile Aurora 1-800-718-7778

Pontiac 1-800-2-PONTIAC

Porsche 1-800-PORSCHE

Saab .... 1-800-582-SAAB Ext 201

Subaru 1-800-WANT-AWD

Suzuki 1-800-650-4445

Toyota............................1-800-GO-TOYOTA

Volkswagen 1-800-DRIVE-VW

Volvo 1-800-960-9988

Travel

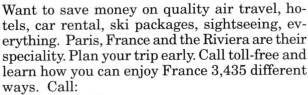

JET VACATIONS

Want to save money on quality air travel, hotels, car rental, ski packages, sightseeing, everything. Paris, France and the Riviera are their speciality. Plan your trip early. Call toll-free and learn how you can enjoy France 3,435 different ways. Call:
1-800-538-0999

BEFORE YOU TRAVEL

Planning a trip? Before you go you'll want to get a copy of *"Lightening The Travel Load Travel Tips"*. This handy booklet is filled with "how-to" materials on selecting, packing, traveling and caring for luggage. Send a card to:
SAMSONITE TRAVELER ADVISORY SERVICE
11200 E. 45TH AVE.
DENVER, CO 80239

TRAVELODGE DIRECTORY

There's a *free directory* of the more than 500 TraveLodge motels and motor hotels waiting for you. It lists location, room rates and a map for each TraveLodge. You'll also find information on their new group rates, family plan and bargain break weekends. Write to:
TRAVELODGE INTERNATIONAL
250 TRAVELODGE DR.
EL CAJON, CA 92090

IMPORTING A CAR

Can you save money by buying a foreign car on your next trip abroad? What are the customs requirements? What should you know about emission standards on a car you import yourself? For answers, drop a card asking for *"Importing A Car"* and *"U.S. Customs Pocket Hints"*. Free from:
U.S. CUSTOMS SERVICE
WASHINGTON, DC 20229

DAYS INNS

Quality accommodations for the American traveler at economical rates has been the motto of Days Inn since its founding in 1970. For a *free directory* of the 301 Inns and 229 Tasty World Restaurants with their rates, maps, toll free numbers and more, call: **1-800-325-2525**

"HOLIDAY INN DIRECTORY"

For a complete listing of Holiday Inns in the U.S. and worldwide request a free copy of their huge directory. In seconds you can locate any of the thousands of Holiday Inns with room rates, list of recreation activities, even a map for each hotel. Call toll free:
1-800-238-8000. OR WRITE:
HOLIDAY INN
3 RAVINIA DR. SUITE 2000
ATLANTA, GA 38195

CLUB MED VACATION

Club Med's unique vacation resorts have de-lighted thousands of people tired of 'the same old thing'. If you're interested in a fun vacation that really is something different, send for the free color *travel booklet* from:
CLUB MED, INC.
3 E. 54TH ST.
NEW YORK, NY 10019
OR CALL: **1-800-CLUB-MED**

BAREFOOT CRUISE

Ready for something different? For a va-cation unlike any you've ever been on, consider sailing a tall ship to a small island in the Caribbean. The full color *"Barefoot Adventure"* will tell you all about 'Barefoot' shipboard adventures aboard schooners that once belonged to Onassis, Vanderbilt and the Duke of Westminster. Call toll free:
1-800-327-2600. OR
SEND A POSTCARD TO:
WINDJAMMER BAREFOOT
CRUISES
BOX 120
MIAMI BEACH, FL 33119

Traveling The USA

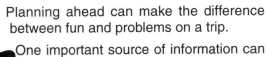

Planning ahead can make the difference between fun and problems on a trip.

One important source of information can be the tourist offices for the states you plan to visit. These offices are set up to provide maps, brochures and other information about the tourist attractions, climate, restaurants and hotels for their states.

When you write to them, specify which areas of the state you plan to visit and indicate any special sight-seeing interests you may have. Often they can provide you with additional materials on the areas that interest you most.

If you plan to tour any part of the U.S.A. write to the tourist offices of each of the 50 states you intend to visit. Be sure to write well in advance of your trip (a postcard will do). The following is a selected list of state tourism offices. If a toll-free 800 number is available, it is given.

ALABAMA
Bureau of Tourism & Travel
P.O. Box 4927
Montgomery, AL 36103-4331
205-242-4169 or 1-800-ALABAMA

ALASKA
Alaska Division of Tourism
P.O. Box 110801
Juneau, AK 99811-0801
907-465 2010

ARIZONA
Arizona Office of Tourism
2702 N. 3RD Street
Suite 4015
Phoenix, AZ 85004
602-542-TOUR

ARKANSAS
Arkansas Department of Parks and Tourism
1 Capitol Mall
Little Rock, AR 72201
501 682-7777 or
1-800-NATURAL

CALIFORNIA
California Office of Tourism
Department of Commerce
301 K Street   Suite 1600
Sacramento, CA 95814
800-862-2543

COLORADO
Colorado Tourism Board
P.O. Box 3524

Englewood, CO 80150
303-592-5410
Ask for a vacation planning kit
call 1-800-433-2656

CONNECTICUT
Tourism Promotion Service
CT Dept. of Economic Development
865 Brook Street
Rocky Hill, CT 06067
203 258-4355 or 800-CT-BOUND (nationwide)

DELAWARE
Delaware Tourism Office
Delaware Development Office
99 Kings Highway
PO. Box 1401
Dover, DE 19903
302-739-4271 or 1-800-441-8846 (both in & out of state)

DISTRICT OF COLUMBIA
Washington Convention and Visitors Association
1212 New York Ave., NW 600
Washington, DC 20005
202-789 7000

FLORIDA
Department of Commerce Visitors Inquiry
126 Van Buren St
Tallahassee, FL 32399-2000
904 487-1462

GEORGIA
Tourist Division
P.O. Box 1776
Atlanta, GA 30301-1776
404-656-3590
1-800 VISIT GA
(1 800 847-4842)

HAWAII
Hawaii Visitors Bureau
2270 Kalakaua Ave.
Suite 801
Honolulu, HI 96815
808-923-1811

IDAHO
Department of Commerce
700 W. State St.
Second Fl.
Boise, ID 83720
208-334-2470 or 1-800-635-7820

ILLINOIS
Illinois Department of Commerce and Community Affairs
Tourist Information Center
310 S. Michigan Ave.
Chicago, IL 60601
312-793-2094

INDIANA
Indiana Dept. of Commerce
Tourism & Film Development Division
One North Capitol
Suite 700
Indianapolis, IN 46204-2288
317-232 8860 or 289-6646

IOWA
Iowa Department of Economic Development Division of Tourism
200 East Grand Avenue
Des Moines, IA 50309
515-242-4705
1-800 345-IOWA

KANSAS
Travel & Tourism Development Division

Department of
Commerce
700 SW Harrison
Topeka, KS 66603-
3712
913-296-2009
1-800-2-KANSAS

KENTUCKY
Department of Travel
Development Dept. MR
PO. Box 2011
Frankfort, KY 40602
1-800-225-TRIP

LOUISIANA
Office of Tourism
PO. Box 94291
Baton Rouge, LA
70804
504-342-8119 or
1-800-33-GUMBO

MAINE
Maine Publicity
Bureau
P.O. Box 2300
Hallowell, ME 04347
207-582-9300

MARYLAND
Office of Tourism
Development
217 E. Redwood St.
Baltimore, MD 21202
1-800-543-1036

MASSACHUSETTS
Executive Office of
Economic Affairs
Office of Travel and
Tourism
100 Cambridge St.,
13th Fl
Boston, MA 02202
617-727-3201

MICHIGAN
Travel Bureau
Department of
Commerce

P.O. Box 30226
Lansing, MI 48909
1-800-5432-YES

MINNESOTA
Minnesota Office of
Tourism
121 7th Place East Suite
100
Metro-Square Bldg.
St. Paul, MN 55101
612-296 5029 or
1-800-657-3700

MISSISSIPPI
Department of
Economic and
Community
Development
Tourism Development
P.O. Box 1705
Ocean Springs, MS
39566
601-359-3297 or
1-800-927-6378

MISSOURI
Missouri Division of
Tourism
Truman State Office
Bldg.
301 W. High St.
PO. Box 1055
Jefferson City, MO
65102
314-751-4133

MONTANA
Department of
Commerce
Travel Montana
1424 9th Avenue
Helena, MT 59620
406-444-2654 or
1-800-541-1447

NEBRASKA
Dept of Economic
Development
Division of Travel and
Tourism

301 Centennial Mall S.
P.O. Box 94666
Lincoln, NE 68509
402-471-3796 or 1-800-228-4307

NEVADA
Commission on
Tourism
Capitol Complex
Carson City, NV 89710
1 800-NEVADA 8

NEW HAMPSHIRE
Office of Vacation
Travel
P.O. Box 856
Concord, NH 03302
603-271-2666 or for
recorded weekly events,
ski conditions, foliage
reports 1-800-258-3608

NEW JERSEY
Division of Travel and
Tourism
20 West State Street
Trenton, NJ 08625
1-800-JERSEY-7

NEW MEXICO
New Mexico Department
of Tourism
Lamy Bldg.
491 Old Santa Fe Trail
Santa Fe, NM 87503
505-827-7400 or
1-800 545-2040

NEW YORK
NYS Tourism
Box 992,
Latham, NY 12110
or call 1-800-CALL NYS

NORTH CAROLINA
Travel and Tourism
Division
Department of
Economic & Community
Development

430 North Salisbury St.
Raleigh, NC 27611
919-733-4171 or
1-800-VISIT NC

NORTH DAKOTA
North Dakota Tourism
Promotion
Liberty Memorial
Building
Capitol Grounds
604 E. Boulevard
Bismarck, ND 58505
701-224 2525 or
1-800-435-5663

OHIO
Ohio Division of Travel
and Tourism
Vern Riffe Center
77 S. High Street
Columbus, OH 43215
1-800 BUCKEYE

OKLAHOMA
Oklahoma Tourism and
Recreation Dept.
Literature Distribution
Center
2401 N. Lincoln Suite
500
Oklahoma City, OK
73105
1-800-652-6552

OREGON
Tourism Division
Oregon Economic
Development Dept.
775 Summer St. NE
Salem, OR 97310
1-800-547-7842

PENNSYLVANIA
Bureau of Travel
Marketing
453 Forum Building
Harrisburg, PA 17120
1-800-VISIT PA, ext. 257

RHODE ISLAND
Rhode Island Tourism
Division
One West Exchange St.
Providence, RI 02903
1-800-556-2484

SOUTH CAROLINA
South Carolina Division
of Tourism
Parks and Recreation
P.O. Box 71
Columbia, SC 29202
1-800-872-3505

SOUTH DAKOTA
Department of Tourism
711 E. Wells Ave.
Pierre, South Dakota
57501

TENNESSEE
Department of Tourist
Development
P.O. Box 23170
Nashville, TN 37202
615-741-2158

TEXAS
Travel Information
Services
Texas Department of
Transportation
P.O. Box 5064
Austin, TX 78763 5064
512-483-3705

UTAH
Utah Travel Council
Council Hall, Capitol Hill
Salt Lake City, UT 84114
801-538 1030

VERMONT
Agency of Development
and Community Affairs
Travel Division
134 State St.
Montpelier, VT 05602
802 828-3236

VIRGINIA
Virginia Department of
Economic Development
Tourism Development
Group
River Front Plaza
West 19th Fl.
Richmond, VA 23219
1-800-VISIT-VA

WASHINGTON
Washington State
Dept. of Trade and
Economic
Development
101 General
Administration Bldg.
P.O. Box 42500
Olympia, WA 98504
206-753-5630

WASHINGTON, D.C.
See District of
Columbia

WEST VIRGINIA
Division of Tourism
and Parks
State Capitol Complex
Bldg. #6 Room #564
1900 Kanawha Blvd.
East
Charleston, WV 25305-
0317
1-800 CALL-WVA

WISCONSIN
Travel Information
Division of Tourism
123 W. Washington
Ave.
P.O. Box 7606
Madison, WI 53707
1-800-432-TRIP

WYOMING
Wyoming Division of
Tourism
I-25 at College Drive
Cheyenne, WY 82002
1-800-225-5996

NATIONAL PARKS

Enjoy the great outdoors. Get back to nature. Visit our beautiful national parks. There's a series of interesting guides to the 7 most popular national parks free for the asking. Send for any (or all) guides you'd like:

"Rocky Mountain National Park, Colorado"
"Mt. McKinley National Park, Alaska"
"Mesa Verde National Park Colorado"
'Hot Springs National Park, Arkansas"
"Hawaii National Park"
"Yellowstone National Park"
"Carlsbad Caverns, New Mexico"..

You might also want the *free map* of the National Park System. Request by name the guides you would like. Write to:

DEPT. OF THE INTERIOR
NATIONAL PARK SERVICE
WASHINGTON, DC 20240

INTERNATIONAL VACATIONLAND— 1000 ISLANDS

The 1000 Islands region features the best of two countries — U.S. and Canada. Some of the many attractions include fishing, golf, tennis, biking, hiking, houseboat rentals, shopping and recreational sports in all seasons. Three tour packages are available for the asking:

1. Write: **1000 Islands, Box 428 Alexandria Bay, NY 13607.** (In Canada write: 1000 Islands, Box 10, Landsdoune, Ontario KOE ILO.

2. Write: **Kingston Bureau of Tourism, Box 486, 209 Ontario St., Kingston, Ontario K7L 2ZI.**

3. Write: **Rideau Lakes Thousand Islands, P.O. Box 125 Perth, Ontario K7H 3E3**

CHOCOLATE TOWN USA

If you are looking for a really fun time, why not

try a special theme weekend at the fun Hershey Park in Hershey, Pennsylvania. For more detailed information, call:
1-800-HERSHEY

Foreign Travel

ANGUILLA
Anguilla Tourist Information,
271 Main Street Northport,
NY 11768

ANTIGUA & BARBUDA
Antigua & Barbuda Dept of
Tourism, 610 Fifth Avenue,
Suite 311, New York, NY 10020

ARGENTINA
For maps and color brochures
describing Argentina drop a card
to: **Argentina Embassy, 1600
New Hampshire Ave., Washington, DC 20009**

ARUBA
Go sailing, scuba diving in the turquoise Caribbean, casinos, discos and lots more. Ask for "Sun Worshippers" with hotel rates and tourist information. Write: **Aruba Tourist Office, 1000 Harbor Boulevard, Weehawken, NJ 07087**

AUSTRIA
Write for the *"Austrian Information package"* and you'll receive a beautiful assortment of travel guides and student education opportunities. Drop a card to: **Austrian National Tourist Office; 500 Fifth Ave., New York. NY 10110**

BAHAMAS
Bahamas Tourist Office: call toll-free 1-800-422-4262

BARBADOS
Discover the many sides of Barbados that make it a luscious vacation spot. A nice tow *package* including several huge wall posters are yours for the asking. Write: **Barbados Board of Tourism, 800 Second Ave., New York, NY 10017**

BELIZE
Belize Tourist Board, 83 North Front Street, PO Box 325, Belize City Belize, Central America

BRITISH VIRGIN ISLANDS
British Tourist Board, 370 Lexington Avenue, New York, NY 10017

BRITAIN
There's always something new to discover in England, Wales, Scotland & Ireland. Drop a card requesting the *Britain Information package* and you'll receive a beautiful color magazine, photos, maps, tours, etc. Send to: **British Tourist Authority, 551 Fifth Ave., New York, NY. Or call: 1-800-462-2748**

BRITAIN BY RAIL
Tour scenic Britain by rail. BritRail offers unlimited travel on most rail, bus & ferry routes. For a free guide travel hints as well as bargain ticket rates write to: **BritRail. Travel International, 1500 Broadway, New York, NY 10017**

BERMUDA
Thinking of traveling to Bermuda? Don't go without this information *package*. It includes travel tips, a map, hotel rates, and more. Write to: **Bermuda Dept. of Tourism. PO Box 77050, Woodside, NY 11377**

CANADA
"Touring Canada" is a big guide to 54 exciting tours of Canada. You'll learn where to go, what to see, what clothes to bring and much more. You'll find there's more to do in 'our neighbor to the north' than you had ever imagined. Write to: **Canadian Government Office of Tourism Ottawa, Canada KIA OH6**

CANCUN & COZUMEL
Cancun & Cozumel Tourist Office, 405 Park Avenue, Suite 1401 New York, NY 10022

CARIBBEAN SUN FUN
Discover the fun and excitement each of the Caribbean islands has to offer. Ask for the *travel package* free from: **Caribbean Tourism Assn., 20 E. 46th St., New York, NY 10017**

CAYMAN ISLANDS
Cayman Islands Tourism, 420 Lexington Avenue, #2733, New York, NY 10170

CHINA - TAIWAN
Taiwan Visitors Association, One World Trade Center, New York, NY

CURACAO
Curacao Tourist Board, 475 Park Ave. South Suite 2000, New York, NY 10016

EGYPT
Travel back in time to the cradle of civilization. Explore the pyramids and discover the old and new wonders of Egypt. Ask for the *Egypt Information package.* Write to: **Egyptian Government Travel Office, 630 Fifth Ave., New York, NY 10111**

FRANCE
The *France Information package* is a mini-tour of France with a large full color tour book plus Paris on a budget, a tour of Paris, hotels and motels in France off-season packages, and more. Drop a card to: **French Government Tourist Office, 444 Madison Ave., New York, NY 10020**

GERMANY
"Welcome To Germany" is a beautiful guide full of color photos that are absolutely breathtaking. This is just part of the Germany Tour package free from: **Lufthansa German Airlines, 1640 Hempstead Turnpike, East Meadow, NY 11554**

GERMANY TRAIN TRAVEL
If you're planning a trip to Germany one of the best ways to tour the country is by train. With German Rail you will have unlimited travel plus discounts on many bus and boat routes. For free information write: **GermanRail, 747 Third Ave., New York, NY 10017**

BERLIN
This city is the Gateway to Continental Europe. You can experience the mix of Berlin's dynamic culture, historic sights and non- stop nightlife. Call for your free *Berlin Travel kit* today. Call **1-800-248-9539**

GREECE
To help you make your trip to Greece more enjoyable, here's a large packet of brochures, maps and booklets on the beautiful Greek Islands. Request the *Greece Tour package* from:

Greek National Tourist Organization, Olympic Tower, 645 Fifth Ave., New York, NY 10022

GRENADA
Grenada Board of Tourism, 820 Second Avenue, Suite 900 D New York, NY 10017

GUYANA
Guyana Tourism, c/o Caribbean Tourism Organization 20 East 46th Street New York, NY 10017-2417

HUNGARY
Like beautiful picture post cards, the color illustrations in this package will take you for a tour of the sights and attractions of Hungary. Ask for the *Hungary Travel package* which includes a map of the country. Send a card to: **Consulate General of Hungarian People's Republic, 8 E. 75th St., New York, NY 10021**

INDIA
Dozens of scenic color photos of India are included in the *India Tour Kit* yours free from: **Information Service of India, Embassy of India, Washington, DC 20008**

INDONESIA
For facts on the Indonesia archipelago including their history, geography, culture, maps, and more drop a card requesting their *information package.* Write to: **Consulate General of Indonesia, Information Section, 5 E. 68th St., New York, NY 10022**

IRELAND
Call: **1-800-SHAMROCK** or write to: **Irish Tourist Board, 345 Park Ave., New York, NY 101 54**

ISRAEL
If you enjoyed the book you'll love the country. For a nice collection of *guide books and maps* of Israel and the Holy Land write to: **Israel Government Tourist Office, 350 Fifth Ave., New York, NY 10118**

ITALY
A beautiful arm chair tour of Italy is in store for you. Write for *"A Trip To Italy tour package"* with road maps and marvelous full color guide books. It's

yours free from: **Italian Government Travel Office, 630 Fifth Ave., New York, NY 10111.**

IVORY COAST

Learn about the rites of Panther Men and the fascinating culture of the Agri Kingdom. All this and much more in the travel kit from: **Ivory Coast Embassy, 2424 Massachusetts Ave. N.W., Washington, DC 20008**

JAMAICA

Soft beaches, jungle waterfalls, hot discos and sailing in the sunshine—it's all in a beautiful full color book that features 56 great vacations. Ask for the free *"Jamaica Vacation Book"* from: **Jamaica Tourist Board, 8237 NW 66th St, Miami, FL 33160**

JAPAN

The *Japan Tour package is* an impressive collection of travel booklets in full color with marvelous illustrations. You'll receive a mini tour of Japan chuck full of facts about Japan's history with travel tips and many fascinating tid bits. For all this write to: **Japanese Tourist Organization, 630 Fifth Ave., New York NY 10111**

MARTINIQUE

Martinique Dept. of Tourism, 610 Fifth Avenue New York, NY 10020

MEXICO

For a set of over a dozen color brochures showing the sights and tourist attractions of Mexico, drop a post card to: **Mexican National Tourist Council, 405 Park Ave., New York, NY 10022**

MONTSERRAT

Montserrat Tourism Information, 485 Fifth Avenue New York, NY 10017

MOROCCO

Exotic Morocco has some of the most magnificent scenery in the world. For a kit of *travel information and tour packages* to this ancient kingdom drop a card to: **Royal Air Maroc, 55 East 59th St., New York, NY**

PORTUGAL

Discover all the beauty of Portugal— its beaches,

entertainment and hotels — all in this package of full color brochures. Call: **TAP Air at 1-800-221-7370.**

PUERTO RICO
Find out why Puerto rico is called "the complete island". There is something here for everyone — sightseeing, sports, night life, casinos and lots more. Call: **1-212-599-6262**

RUSSIA
Write to: **Embassy of The Russian Federation, 1125 16th St. N.W., Washington, D.C. 20036**

ST. MAARTEN
For beautiful travel brochures of the island of St. Maarten call: **1-800-ST-MAARTEN**

SCOTLAND
For colorful brochures on Scotland, call toll-free: **1-800-343-SCOT**

SINGAPORE
Singapore's the place where all Asia comes together. Here's a beautiful color package of things to do and see plus a map and even a recipe booklet with delightful meals of Singapore. Write to: **Embassy of Republic of Singapore, 1824 'R' St. N.W., Washington, D.C. 20009**

SOUTH AFRICA
Write to: **Embassy of South Africa, 3501 Massachusetts Ave. N.W., Washington, D.C. 20008**

SPAIN
Write to: **Spain Office of Tourism, 666 Fifth Ave, New York, NY 10103**

SWITZERLAND
For a mini-tour of the Alps send a postcard for the *Swiss Tour package.* You'll receive beautifully illustrated booklets, maps, travel tips, recipes and more. All of this comes to you free from: **Swiss National Tourist Office, 608 Fifth Ave., New York, NY 10020**

THAILAND
Come to Thailand and enjoy its dazzling scenery, incredible shopping bargains and the special joy of sharing all they have. Drop a card to: **Tourism Authority of Thailand, 3440 Wilshire Blvd., Suite 1101, Los Angeles, CA 90010. Or: Tour-**

ism Authority of Thailand, 5 World Trade Center, Suite 2449, New York, NY 10048

U.S. VIRGIN ISLANDS
For great duty-free shopping consider the U.S. Virgin Islands for your next vacation. No passports are needed, their language is English and they use U.S. currency. For full *travel information* write: **U.S. Virgin Islands Tourism, 1270 Avenue of the Americas, New York, NY 10020**

ZAMBIAN SAFARI
Zambia has a big package of travel & tourist information waiting for you. The beautiful color brochures are a mini-safari through the African bush. Write to: **Zambia National Tourist Office, 237 E. 52nd St., New York, NY 10022**

PERU AND NATURE
Here are colorful maps, charts and pictures of native birds, flowers and animals. You'll also find a listing of national parks and reserves, as well as interesting archaeological and historical highlights. Write to:
**EXPLORATIONS, INC.
27655 KENT RD.
BONITA SPRINGS, FL 33923**

HONG KONG TOURIST INFORMATION
If you are over 60 years old and are thinking of going on a shopping trip to Hong Kong, there's a free discount booklet that will save you money on your shopping. Write to:
**HONG KONG TOURIST INFORMATION
590 FIFTH AVE.
NEW YORK, NY 10036**

NOVA SCOTIA, CANADA
"Nova Scotia Holiday" is a beautiful color book that tells all about things to see, history, legends, customs crafts and more. Call toll-free: **800-341-6096** or write to: **Nova Scotia Information. P.O. Box 130 Halifax. Nova Scotia, Canada B3J 2M7**

Money Matters

MONEY FACTS

The federal Reserve Bank of Atlanta has a free booklet that describes how currency is designed, printed, circulated and eventually destroyed. There's even a section on how to redeem damaged bills. Ask for *"Fundamental Facts about U.S. Money."* Write to:

FEDERAL RESERVE BANK
OF ATLANTA
PUBLIC AFFAIRS DEPT.
ATLANTA, GA. 30303

FAST BANKING

The American Bankers Association's free brochure on *"A Dozen Ways to Save Time and Money at the Bank"* offers a variety of tips on money management. For a free copy, write to:

ATTENTION: 'A DOZEN TIPS.'
THE AMERICAN BANKERS ASSOCIATION
1120 CONNECTICUT AVE. N.W.
WASHINGTON, D.C. 20036

"CHOOSING THE MORTGAGE THAT'S RIGHT FOR YOU"

Ready to shop for a mortgage? This easy to read 40 page guide can help. It walks you through the mortgage shopping process in three easy steps. How big a mortgage loan you can afford, choosing a mortgage that's right for you, and comparing terms among lenders. This guide is free from:

FANNIE MAE
PO BOX 27463
RICHMOND, VA 23286-8999
OR CALL 1-800 688-HOME

FINANCIAL ADVISER

Everybody, regardless of age, should have a financial adviser. Just remember it's never to late to build a nest egg. Oppenheimer Funds Inc. has published a guide *"Finding A Financial Adviser Who's Right For You."* This will take you through the process step by step of selecting names, conducting interviews, making the final decision, and maintaining a relationship that will be profitable. This is a must for anyone looking for help in making intelligent financial planning decisions. To order your free copy call: **1-800 525-7048.**

"TAX DO'S & DON'TS FOR MUTUAL FUND INVESTORS"

This 20 page brochure list 13 points to consider about the tax aspects of mutual fund investing. For example , it warns you *not* to assume that all fund distributions are the same, that you owe no taxes on reinvested dividends or that you owe no tax if you exchange shares from one fund for shares of another in mutual fund 'families.' For a copy of the free brochure write to:
ICI
1401 H ST. N.W., SUITE 1200
WASHINGTON, D.C. 2005

INVESTING FOR RETIREMENT

"IRA Transfers" is a free brochure that tax-sheltered retirement investing. It can help you get the most from your investments. It is published by the AARP Investment Program from Scudder, Stevens & Clark - a group of no-load mutual funds designed for members of the AARP, but open to investors of any age. (No load means there is no sales commission.) For a copy, call: **1-(800) 322 2282, EXT. 8271**

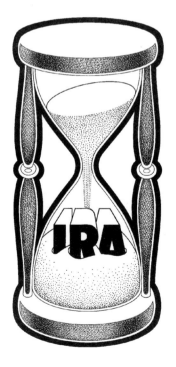

"The State Tax Laws: A Guide for Investors Aged 50 and Over" is another free publication from AARP. Scudder prepared this 112 page guide in conjunction with the National Conference of State Legislatures. For a copy call: **1(800-322-2282, EXT 8254**

TAXES

When tax time comes around it's always a good

idea to have a tax pro help you. For the names of tax experts in your area, call the National Association of Enrolled Agents: **1-800 424-4339**

NEW VENTURE

If you are thinking of going into business and starting a new corporation, here's a booklet you will definitely want to get. *Starting Your Own Corporation* will answer many of the questions you may have regarding setting up the right kind of corporation. For your free copy, call the "Corporation Company" at **1-800-542-2677.**

PERSONAL FINANCE HELPLINES

If you are not sure where to turn for good advice regarding your personal finances, here are several toll-free hotlines you can turn to for help. They will either provide you with the information you need or they will tell you where you can go for further assistance.

FINANCIAL PLANNING

THE INSTITUTE OF CERTIFIED FINANCIAL PLANNERS – FOR BROCHURES & REFERRALS, CALL **1-800-282-7526**
THE AMERICAN INSTITUTE OF CERTIFIED PUBLIC ACCOUNTANTS' PERSONAL FINANCIAL PLANNING DIVISION CALL: **(1-800) 862- 4272**
THE INTERNATIONAL ASSOCIATION FOR FINANCIAL PLANNING CALL: **(404) 395-1605** (NOT TOLL-FREE)
THE NATIONAL ASSOCIATION OF PERSONAL FINANCIAL ADVISERS CALL: **1-800 366-2732**
THE AMERICAN SOCIETY OF CLU AND CHFC CALL: **1-800-392-6900**

INVESTMENTS

To find a stockbroker, ask for referrals from friends, relatives, professional acquaintenances. To check a broker's background, call:
THE NATIONAL ASSOCIATION OF SECURITIES DEALERS: **1-800-289-9999**

SOCIAL SECURITY

For an estimate of what your retirement benefits might be call: **1-800-772-1213** and ask for an *'earnings estimate request'* to fill out and return.

CURRENCY SAVERS

Did your dog chew up some money you left on the table? Well the U.S. Department of Treasury can help restore that money for you. Drop them a line with a plausible detailed explanation. Once the claim is processsed the actual payment is made by federal check. For more information write:

U.S. DEPARTMENT OF THE TREASURY
OFFICE OF CURRENCY STANDARDS
15TH STREET & PENNSYLVANIA AVE., N.W.
WASHINGTON, D.C. 20220
OR CALL (1-202) 622-2000

MORTGAGES

If you are looking for a new mortgage but are not sure what you should do to get the mortgage that is best for you, there's a toll-free number to First Financial Equity you can call for more information and for answers to your questions. Call:

1-800-454-0505

INVESTMENTS

Before you make any significant investment, learn what to look for to find the one that's best for you. Also discover how to evaluate your investment and determine how well it meets your objectives. Ask for *"Evaluating Investment Performance"* write to:

NEUBERGER & BERMAN
INDIVIDUAL ASSET MANAGEMENT GROUP
605 THIRD AVE.
NEW YORK, NY 10158
OR CALL 800-234-9840

OVER 50?

Now that a large portion of the population is over 50 years old, there are lots of bargains and discounts available just for the asking. Remember if you don't ask you'll never know. Always check to see if there are certain days or certain times when seniors are offered discounts or specials. Many hotels offer discounts on their rooms as well as disounts if you eat in their restaurants. You can also apply for a travel club card if you are a member of AARP...The American Association of Retired People.

MUTUAL FUNDS

Learn all about mutual funds and find out which are the best ones for you. Check out the Strong Equity Performers from Dreyfus call: **1-800 THE LION** ext 4043 or visit a Dreyfus Financial Center via the Internet: **http://www.dreyfus.com/funds**

GLOBAL UTILITIES FUND

Basic utilities such as water and electricity are always in demand and telecommunications is growing in all countries. That's why the Franklin Global Utilities Fund could be a growth fund for you. They will manage a portfolio especially designed for you. If this sounds like something you would consider, call today for a free brochure: **1-800 342-Fund** or write:

FRANKLIN FUNDS
777 MARINERS ISLAND BOULEVARD
SAN MATEO, CA 94404-1585

LOW INSURANCE PREMIUMS

If you are in the market for Medicare and Medigap policies for health insurance for yourself or a parent, your premiums will be lowest if you enroll from three months before, to four months after your 65th birthday. After that, the premiums may grow by 10 percent each year you wait. For more information, call **1-800-772-1213** and ask for The Social Security Administration's free *"Guide to Health Insurance for People with Medicare"* or write:

THE HEALTH INSURANCE ASSOCIATION OF AMERICA
PUBLICATION OFFICE
555 13TH ST. N. W.
SUITE 600-E
WASHINGTON, D.C. 20004

MUTUAL FUNDS FOR INVESTORS OVER 50

"Understanding Mutual Funds: A Guide for Investors Aged 50"and Over", defines the basics to help older individuals choose funds appropriate for their needs. Absolutely free! Write:

AARP INVESTMENT PROGRAM
SCUDDER PROCESSING CENTER
BOX 5014
JANESVILLE, WI 53547.
OR CALL: 800-322-2282, EXT 4884

MUTUAL FUNDS

To find out more about money market funds, contact one or more of these large funds for their *prospectus and information package:*

DREYFUS SERVICE CORP.
600 MADISON AVE.
NEW YORK, NY 10022.

FIDELITY CASH RESERVES
P.O. BOX 832
BOSTON, MA 02103.
CALL 800-225-6190.
(IN MA CALL COLLECT 617-523-1919.)

IDS CASH MANAGEMENT FUND
P.O. BOX 369
MINNEAPOLIS, MN 55440.
CALL 1-800-437-4332

TAX-FREE INCOME FUND

You can start earning tax-free income with as little as $1,000 with prompt liquidity and no sales or redemption fee. Call: **1-800-638-5660**

FUND RAISING

If your school or organization needs money, this *free fund-raising kit* will teach you how. This kit will help show your group how to collect member's recipes and publish them into a great cookbook. Write for your free kit to:

FUNDCRAFT
410 HIGHWAY 72 W.
BOX 340
COLLIERVILLE, TN 38017

BE YOUR OWN BROKER

If you have a computer and like to make your own investment decisions without the help of a stockbroker, this one may be for you. Charles Schwab has free computer software you can use to buy and sell securities over the internet for just $29.95 for up to 1,000 shares. The software also allows you to do your own research using various internet databases, track the stocks you are interested in and lots more. For more information call: **1-800-E-SCHWAB.**

IRS OR H & R BLOCK?

Few people realize that the IRS is committed to giving taxpayers every legitimate deduction they're entitled to. The IRS has toll-free numbers throughout the country you can call for assistance and/or forms. The Internal Revenue Service tax hotline for answers to your income tax question is:
1-800-829-1040

The IRS also has a series of helpful publications such as *"Federal Income Tax"* available free of charge. Call the toll-free number for this publication or a list of the others available.

The IRS even has a toll-free number to assist deaf/hearing-impaired taxpayers who have access to TV-Phone/Teletypewriter equipment (800-428-4732; In Indiana — 800-382-4059).

1040

Free From The U.S. Government

PERSONAL EARNINGS & BENEFIT ESTIMATE STATEMENT

This statement tells how much Social Security earnings-year by year- have been reported by your employers, and what your benefits will be if you retire at different ages. Find out what disability benefits you qualify for... and how the value of your benefits compares with the amount of Social Security taxes you have paid. This is free from the Social Security Administration. Call:
1-800-772-1213

MISSING PERSONS

If you have a problem of trying to locate a missing relative or friend, a letter to the Social Security Administration may help. When you write be sure to include as much information as you can about the missing person (including their last address and date of birth). Write to:
PUBLIC INQUIRIES
SOCIAL SECURITY ADMINISTRATION
6501 SECURITY BLVD.
BALTIMORE, MD 20235

STRIKING IT RICH

Did you know that the U.S. Government will let you prospect on public lands? If you would like to find out how to strike it rich on government lands, send a card to the Forest Service. Also ask for *"A Guide To Your National Forests."* Write:
MINERALS AND GEOLOGY STAFF
FOREST SERVICE, DOA
BOX 2417
WASHINGTON, DC 20013

BUYING U.S. GOVERNMENT SURPLUS

The U.S. Government must sell surplus property of all types on a regular basis. To find out how to buy everything from binoculars to autos at bargain prices write to:

SURPLUS SALES CENTER
WASHINGTON NAVY YARD
WASHINGTON, DC 20408

FREE FIREWOOD

In most of the 154 National Forests firewood for your own personal use, is free. To find out how you can get free firewood and also how to select, purchase and use firewood ask for "Firewood Information." Free from:

FIREWOOD #559,
FOREST SERVICE
BOX 2417
WASHINGTON, DC 20013

JOBS

Various branches of the Federal Government have positions open throughout the U.S. The majority of these jobs are in large metropolitan areas. Drop them a card and ask for *"Job Information"*. Write:

OFFICE OF PERSONNEL MANAGEMENT
PO BOX 52
WASHINGTON, D.C. 20044

SAVINGS BOND REDEMPTION

Every Series E Savings Bond ever issued (since 1941) is still earning interest. If you own any bonds and would like to know exactly how much they're worth today, write for *"Tables of Redemption Values For $25 Series E Savings Bonds"* from:

BUREAU OF PUBLIC DEBT
PARKERSBURG, WV 26101

HELP FOR CONSUMERS

What can you do to protect yourself and your family against unsafe products? The first thing you can do is call the Consumer Product Safety Commission's toll-free hotline. They monitor product safety and product recalls. For example, the commission can tell you if your hair dryer

has asbestos lining. They have over 90 safety fact sheets on a variety of products. For the kids there are free comic books on poison and bicycle safety and coloring books on toys and play-ground safety. For more information call:
1-800-638-8326

SECRET SERVICE

The Secret Service does more than protect the President. It was originally created to suppress counterfeiting - a job they still perform - Ask for *"Counterfeiting and Forgery"* which shows how to detect a counterfeit bill. Write to:
U.S. SECRET SERVICE
1800 'G' ST. N.W., ROOM 941
WASHINGTON, DC 20223

CRIME RESISTANCE

The F.B.I. would like every family to feel more secure. Learn how to better protect your family against crime. *"A Way to Protect Your Family Against Crime"* offers tips you and your family can safely use to take a bite out of crime. Ask for the free Crime Resistance booklet. You might also want a copy of *"Abridged History of the F.B.I."* All free from:

PUBLIC AFFAIRS DEPT.
F.B.I.
10TH & PENNSYLVANIA AVE.
WASHINGTON, DC 20535

BUYING U.S. GOVERNMENT SECURITIES

Americans have been buying Series E Savings bonds for many years. But few know they can buy Treasury Bonds and Bills that pay even higher interest. For more information on how you can get in on this no-risk, high-yield investment, write for *U.S. Securities Available to Investors.* From:
PUBLIC DEBT INFORMATION
U.S. DEPARTMENT OF THE TREASURY
WASHINGTON, D.C. 20226

Consumer Information From The U.S. Government

Agencies of the U.S. Government publish thousands of documents every year. While many are too technical for general interest, others are of interest to a wide number of consumers. Those that are, are available through:

CONSUMER INFORMATION, PUEBLO CO 81002

All of the publications listed here are either free or $1.00 or less (for s&h). You can receive up to 25 free publications by simply enclosing $1.00 as a processing fee. (See more complete details at the end of this section.)

CARS

GLOVE BOX TIPS

Five booklets to help you get your car ready for summer and winter driving, choose the right repair shop, and get the best work from your mechanic. 10 pp. **# 302D. 50¢.**

HOW TO FIND YOUR WAY UNDER THE HOOD & AROUND THE CAR

Instructions for 14 preventative maintenance services you can perform on your car. 2 pp. **# 303D. 50¢.**

HOW TO GET A GREAT DEAL ON A NEW CAR

Step-by-step instructions for a proven negotiation technique that you can use to save money on your next car. 4 pp. **# 304D. 50¢.**

New Car Buying Guide

Discusses pricing terms, financing options, and various contracts. Includes a worksheet to help you bargain. 2 pp. **# 305D. 50¢.**

NINE WAYS TO LOWER YOUR AUTO INSURANCE COSTS

Tips on what to do to lower your expenses. Includes a chart to compare discounts. 6 pp. **# 306D. 50¢.**

UNDERHOOD TIPS TO HELP YOU KEEP YOUR COOL

Learn how non-Freon air conditioners affect you and the environment. 2 pp. **# 502D. Free.**

CHILDREN - LEARNING ACTIVITIES

DEPUTY FIRE MARSHAL KIT

Stickers, a badge, and colorful certificate teach elementary age children the school rules of fire safety. **# 504D. Free.**

Helping Your Child Learn Geography
Revised. Teach 5 - 10 year old children geography in ways that are challenging and fun. 36 pp. **# 372D. 50¢**

Helping Your Child Learn History
Makes history interesting to 4-11 year olds with lots of activities and fun things to do. 50 pp. **# 307D. 50¢.**

Helping Your Child Learn Math
26 meaningful and fun activities to help your children (ages 5-13) see math as a positive and interesting part of life. 64 pp. **# 308D. 50¢.**

Helping Your Child Learn to Read
Activities to help you and your child (10 years and under) develop a strong foundation for reading. Good for older children too. 65 pp. **# 309D. 50¢.**

Helping Your Child Succeed in School
Fifteen fun activities to do with your children (ages 5-11) to help expand their imagination, obey, organize, help others, and more. 52 pp. **# 311D. 50¢.**

Helping Your Child With Homework
Suggestions to help you help your child set the time and place for homework, follow-up with the teacher, and more. Good for grades K-9. 48 pp. **# 312D. 50¢.**

Timeless Classics
Lists nearly 400 books published before 1960 for children of all ages. Divided in grade groups of kindergarten through 12th. 2 pp. **# 314D. 50¢.**

JR. HIGH & BEYOND

All About Direct Loans
Learn about the four types of direct student education loans, how much you can borrow, how to apply, how you'll be paid once you're approved, repayment options and your rights and responsibilities. 33 pp. **# 516D. Free.**

Catch the Spirit
A Student's Guide to Community Service. Describes volunteer opportunities, along with local

and national resources for more information. 15 pp. **#503D. Free.**

DIRECT STUDENT LOAN CONSOLIDATION
This could benefit you financially. Learn how to consolidate your federal loans into a single Direct Loan Account, your options for repayment, and more. 16 pp.**# 517D. Free.**

ELECTRONIC APPLICATION FOR FEDERAL STUDENT AID
Two 3.5" diskettes with software (Windows compatible), extensive on-line instructions, and a user guide so that you can fill out and send your application for federal student aid directly to the schools you're applying to. Use with any IBM compatible PC with a modem. **# 615D. Free.**

PLANNING FOR COLLEGE
Strategies to help you plan for tuition and fees along with helpful charts for estimating future costs. 10 pp. **# 507D. Free.**

PREPARING YOUR CHILD FOR COLLEGE
A Resource Book for Parents. Work sheets and checklists to help plan for college academically and financially. Gives examples of typical college costs, suggests ways to save, and much more. 57 pp. **# 508D. Free.**

THE REAL DEAL
Word games, a poster, and puzzles to help junior high students learn to be smart consumers. 12 pp. **#313D. 50¢.**

PARENTING

BABY SAFETY CHECKLIST
Keep this growth chart handy to mark and date your baby's development and review the 12 important safety tips. **#315D. 50¢.**

GROWING UP DRUG FREE
Shows parents what children should know about drugs, including alcohol and tobacco, at each age level. 33 pp. **#505D. Free.**

HOW TO GIVE MEDICINE TO CHILDREN
Five questions to ask the pharmacist, and tips on safely using dosing aids. 4 pp. **#616D. Free.**

KIDS AREN'T JUST SMALL ADULTS
Important information about giving nonprescription medicine to your children. 1 pp. **# 506D. Free.**

KIDS' VACCINATIONS GET A LITTLE EASIER
Learn what they are and how they work to keep your child healthy. Includes a vaccination schedule. 5 pp.**#553D. Free.**

LEARNING DISABILITIES
Explains the differences between learning problems and disabilities. A chart shows language and reasoning skills to watch for at different ages and more. 40 pp. **#316D. 50¢.**

PREVENTING CHILDHOOD POISONING
How to spot symptoms of poisoning, and what antidotes to give. 4 pp. **#509D. Free.**

SCHOOLS WITHOUT DRUGS
An action plan for parents, teachers, school administrators, and students that can help fight drug use. 91 pp. **#510D. Free.**

TOYS & PLAY
Learn how play can improve your child's development. Includes a toy safety and buying guide for children up to 12 years old. 23 pp. # **511D. Free.**

EMPLOYMENT

THE GED DIPLOMA
Learn what the General Education Development Diploma tests cover, how to prepare, and where to get more information. 16 pp # **512D. Free.**

HANDY REFERENCE GUIDE TO THE FAIR LABOR STANDARDS ACT
Revised. Explains the federal laws on minimum wage, overtime pay, record-keeping, child labor, and more. 18 pp. # **374D. 50¢.**

HEALTH BENEFITS UNDER COBRA (CONSOLIDATED OMNIBUS BUDGET RECONCILIATION ACT)
How to keep or buy coverage for yourself and family after a job loss, reduced work hours, divorce, or death. 24 pp. # **317D. 50¢.**

HIGH EARNING WORKERS WHO DON'T HAVE A BACHELOR'S DEGREE
Lists more than 100 occupations requiring less than a college degree. 8 pp. **#101D. $1.00.**

HOW TO FILE A CLAIM FOR YOUR BENEFITS
Here's what to do if your claim or appeal for health, disability, or severance benefits is denied. Covers what the law does, waiting periods, and

more. 2 pp **#318D. 50¢.**

OSHA- EMPLOYEE WORKPLACE RIGHTS.

What to do if you question the safety of, and/or hazards in the workplace. Gives addresses and phone numbers of various federal and state offices to contact for more information or help. 19 pp. **# 617D. Free.**

RESUMES, APPLICATION FORMS, COVER LETTERS, AND INTERVIEWS

Tips on tailoring your resume for specific jobs and sample interview questions. 8 pp. **#102D. $1.00.**

WHAT YOU SHOULD KNOW ABOUT YOUR PENSION RIGHTS

An explanation of your rights, information about benefits, payment schedules, protections, and more. 48 pp. **# 359D. 50¢.**

YOUR GUARANTEED PENSION

Answers 19 frequently asked questions about the security of private pension plans, including benefits and plan termination. 11 pp.**# 596D. Free**.

ENVIRONMENT

COLLECTING USED OIL FOR RECYCLING/REUSE

Tips for changing your own motor oil and explains why recycling oil helps the environment and saves energy. 2 pp. **# 513D. Free.**

COOLING YOUR HOME NATURALLY

Suggests how to save electricity and keep your home cool with landscaping, roof treatments, and more. 8 pp. **#104D. $1.00.**

THE DUCK STAMP STORY

Help preserve wetlands and wildlife refuges by becoming a collector of these unique stamps. 2 pp. **#514D. Free.**

ENERGY-EFFICIENT WINDOWS

Describes how to reduce your home's heating, cooling, and lighting costs. 6 pp. **#105D. $1.00.**

HEALTHY LAWN, HEALTHY ENVIRONMENT

Tips on soil preparation, grasses, watering, mowing, pesticides, choosing a lawn care service, and more. 19 pp.**# 319D. 50¢.**

WHY SAVE ENDANGERED SPECIES?

Ways to get involved in saving plants and animals 7 pp. **# 515D. Free.**

FEDERAL PROGRAMS

THE AMERICANS WITH DISABILITIES ACT
Questions and Answers. Explains how the civil rights of persons with disabilities are protected at work and in public places. 32 pp. **#602D. Free.**

ARE THERE ANY PUBLIC LANDS FOR SALE?
Describes the federal program to sell excess undeveloped public land and why there is no more available for homesteading. 12 pp. **#106D. $1.00.**

HOW YOU CAN BUY USED FEDERAL PERSONAL PROPERTY

The government sells its used equipment and industrial items; here are telephone numbers to call for more information. 4 pp. **# 320D. 50¢.**

U.S. REAL PROPERTY SALES LIST
Lists government properties for sale that are sold by auction or sealed bid. Tells how to get more information. 5 pp.**# 519D. Free.**

YOUR SOCIAL SECURITY NUMBER
Explains why we have social security numbers, when and how to get one, and how to protect its privacy. 2 pp.**# 520D. Free.**

BENEFITS

MEDICARE COVERS MAMMOGRAMS
Describes what a mammogram is, how it detects early breast cancer, and what Medicare covers. 5 pp.**# 521D. Free.**

MEDICARE MANAGED CARE
Compares the benefits and disadvantages of managed care vs. fee-for-service plans. Lists phone numbers of state health insurance offices for information and counseling. 19 pp.**# 610D. Free.**

MEDICARE PAYS FOR FLU SHOTS
Why, when, and where Medicare recipients can get free flu shots. 2 pp.**# 522D. Free.**

REQUEST FOR EARNINGS AND BENEFIT ESTIMATE STATEMENT.
A form to complete and return to Social Security to get your earnings history and an estimate of future benefits. 3 pp. **# 523D. Free.**

SOCIAL SECURITY
Understanding the Benefits. Explains retire-

ment, disability, survivor's benefits, Medicare coverage, Supplemental Security Income, and more. 40 pp.# **524D. Free.**

SOCIAL SECURITY
What Every Woman Should Know. What women should know about benefits upon retirement, disability, widowhood, or divorce. 17 pp. # **618D. Free.**

FOOD & NUTRITION

ACTION GUIDE FOR HEALTHY EATING
Practical ideas to help you lower your risk of cancer by eating less fat and more fruits, vegetables, and whole grains. 16 pp. # **525D. Free.**

CAN YOUR KITCHEN PASS THE FOOD SAFETY TEST?
Take the 10 point quiz on food storage, handling, and cooking to protect your family from foodborne illnesses. 4 pp. **#526D. Free.**

A CONSUMER'S GUIDE TO FATS
Describes the different types of fats and cholesterol and their effects on your health. Includes a glossary of common "fat words." 5 pp.# **527D. Free.**

DIETARY GUIDELINES FOR AMERICANS
How to choose a diet that will taste good, be nutritious, and reduce chronic disease risks. 43 pp.# **321D. 50¢.**

FOOD ALLERGIES: RARE BUT RISKY
Learn the differences between food allergies and food intolerance; diagnosis and tips on preventing and treating allergic reactions. 6 pp. **#528D. Free.**

FOOD LABEL CLOSE-UP
Describes the new food label requirements, including nutrition facts, ingredients, nutrient content, health claims, and the value of package dates. 5 pp. **#529D. Free.**

A FRESH LOOK AT FOOD PRESERVATIVES
Describes how and why food preservatives are used and what safety standards are followed. 5 pp # **530D. Free.**

GROWING OLDER, EATING BETTER
How and why to follow a nutritious diet as you grow older. Lists sources of information about meal programs and available assistance. 5 pp. # **531D. Free.**

HEALTHFUL SNACKS FOR THE CHIP & DIP CROWD

Tips on choosing what snacks are best for you and your diet. Also discusses the new fat-based substitute Olestra which adds no fat or calories. 5 pp. **#532D. Free.**

How to Buy Fruits, Vegetables, and Meats
Use these tips to make healthy decisions based on nutritive value, prices, wholesomeness, quality, and convenience:

How to Buy Fresh Fruits. 26 pp. **#322D.50¢**
How to Buy Fresh Vegetables 26 pp. **#323D. 50¢.**
How to Buy Meat 22 pp. **# 324D. 50¢.**

Is Something Fishy Going On?
Explains names and appearance of different species of fish so you can spot some of the most common sales frauds. 5 pp. **# 533D. Free.**

Making It Easier to Shed Pounds
The New Food Label. Helps the diet-conscious select nutritious foods for their weight-loss plan. 6 pp. **# 534D. Free.**

Quick Consumer Guide to Safe Food Handling
Avoid food poisoning by learning how long some foods can be safely frozen or refrigerated. 8 pp. **#535D. Free.**

Scouting for Sodium
The New Food Label. Gives tips on how to use the new food label in choosing foods for a low-sodium diet. 5 pp. **# 536D. Free.**

Taking the Fat Out of Food
Describes various fat substitutes that can make your diet healthier. Sample menu to cut your fat intake by 50%. 6 pp. **#538D. Free.**

Talking About Turkey
How to buy, store, thaw, stuff, and prepare turkey. A complete guide with recipes and charts. 22 pp. **# 539D. Free.**

HEALTH

Fighting Fleas and Ticks
How to remove a tick safely, prevent tick-borne disease, and tips on keeping fleas away. 6 pp. **#540D. Free.**

Guide to Choosing a Nursing Home
When to visit, whom to talk to, and what to ask about quality care, payment, Medicare/Medicaid coverage, and other insurance. Includes a helpful checklist. 19 pp. **# 541D. Free.**

HEALTH INFORMATION ON-LINE
Access to virtually limitless health and medical information is available on the Internet, including fraudulent and false information. Suggestions to help determine if a site is reliable and where to find reputable sites. 5 pp. **#613D. Free.**

LIFTING THE CLOUDS OF CATARACTS
Discusses how cataracts develop, symptoms and treatment options, including intraocular lens implants. 4 pp. **#543D. Free.**

PROGRESS IN BLOOD SUPPLY SAFETY
Discusses how the blood industry is regulated, and the tests now performed on all donated blood. 4 pp. **# 544D. Free.**

QUESTIONS TO ASK YOUR DOCTOR BEFORE YOU HAVE SURGERY
With follow-up information to help you make decisions about your health care. 14 pp.**#115D. $1.00.**

SEVEN STEPS TO SAFER SUNNING
Practical tips to help you assess your risk of skin damage. Monthly skin self-examination chart included. 5 pp. **#619D. Free.**

SILICONE BREAST IMPLANTS
Where to get more information, report problems, and precautions to take if you already have implants. 4 pp. **# 545D. Free.**

THE SUN, UV, AND YOU
Explains what the UV (ultraviolet radiation) index is and how you can use it to avoid skin cancer, cataracts, and premature aging of the skin. Gives special information for children. 12 pp. **#546D. Free.**

WALKING FOR EXERCISE AND PLEASURE
Includes illustrated warm-up exercises and advice on how far, how fast, and how often to walk for best results. 14 pp. **#116D. $1.00.**

DRUGS & HEALTH AIDS

ASPIRIN
A New Look at an Old Drug. How aspirin can help in the prevention and treatment of cardiovascular disease. 3 pp. **#547D. Free.**

BUYING MEDICINE?
Help Protect Yourself Against Tampering. 1 pp. **#548D. Free**.

CHOOSING MEDICAL TREATMENTS
Describes how to decide if alternative therapy such as acupuncture, hypnosis, herbs, or biofeedback, is right for you. How to avoid fraudulent health treatments. 5 pp.# **549D. Free**.

DEPO-PROVERA
Discusses benefits and risks of this injection that prevents pregnancy for three months. 3 pp. # **550D. Free.**

EYE WEAR
Tells what different eye specialists do and gives questions to ask when shopping for eyeglasses or contact lenses. 2 pp. # **325D. 50¢.**

FDA's TIPS FOR TAKING MEDICINES
How to get the most benefit with fewest risks. Questions to ask and suggestions for long-term medication use. 5 pp. # **551D. Free.**

HOCUS-POCUS AS APPLIED TO ARTHRITIS
Discusses fraudulent cures and medically sound treatments for arthritis, rheumatism, and gout. 4 pp.# **552D. Free.**

MAKING IT EASIER TO READ PRESCRIPTIONS
Gives example of a typical prescription and lists common symbols and terms so you can understand your doctor's instructions. 3 pp. #**554D. Free.**

MAMMOGRAPHY FACILITIES MUST MEET QUALITY STANDARDS
Learn what has changed to better your chances of early detection of breast tumors. 5 pp. # **555D. Free.**

NONPRESCRIPTION MEDICINES
What's Right for You? Important advice on choosing over-the-counter (OTC) medicines and avoiding harmful interactions. 12 pp. # **556D. Free.**

NOT A CURE-ALL, EYE SURGERY HELPS SOME SEE BETTER
Discusses and compares common surgical procedures and the new laser procedures. 5 pp. # **557D. Free.**

TAMING TUMMY TURMOIL
Lists over-the-counter medications (and their possible side effects) for motion sickness, heartburn, indigestion and overindulgence. 4 pp.# **559D. Free.**

UNPROVEN MEDICAL TREATMENTS LURE ELDERLY

Americans spend nearly $20 billion each year on unproven medical treatments. Learn why these can be dangerous and how to avoid fraud. 5 pp.# **560D. Free.**

MEDICAL PROBLEMS

ALZHEIMER'S DISEASE
Is a group of diseases that lead to the loss of mental and physical functions. Learn how Alzheimer's is diagnosed, possible causes, and current treatments. Lists references and sources for more help. 36 pp. **#561D. Free.**

CHRONIC FATIGUE SYNDROME
Learn the symptoms and what treatments are being studied. 15 pp. **#326D. 50¢.**

COPING WITH ARTHRITIS IN ITS MANY FORMS
Describes proven treatments for the most common types of arthritis, and how to avoid being a target for fraudulent "cures." 5 pp. # **562D. Free.**

DON'T LOSE SIGHT OF GLAUCOMA
Glaucoma is a leading cause of blindness. Find out who is most likely to develop it, what the symptoms are, and how it is treated. 2 pp. **#327D. 50¢.**

Preventing Stroke
Discusses what a stroke is, warning signs, and risk factors. Includes a chart to estimate your stroke risk. 8 pp. **#375D. 50¢.**

PROSTATE CANCER
is the second most common cancer in men. Learn how it's detected, what treatments are available, and where to get more information. 5 pp. # **563D. Free.**

SPREAD THE WORD ABOUT CANCER
A Guide for Black Americans. Learn what you can do to reduce your chances of getting cancer. 12 pp. **#564D. Free.**

URINARY TRACT INFECTIONS IN ADULTS
Discusses the risks, symptoms, and treatments of this common and frequent infection. 19 pp. # **328D. 50¢.**

VARICOSE VEIN TREATMENTS
Explains various treatments, risks and side effects; questions to ask your doctor; and warnings about fraudulent claims. 2 pp.# **329D. 50¢.**

WHEN THE SPINE CURVES
How to detect and get help treating scoliosis, an abnormal curvature of the spine that may show up during adolescence. 3 pp. **#565D. Free.**

YEAST INFECTIONS
Describes the symptoms, causes, available medications, and preventive tips. 2 pp. **# 566D. Free.**

MENTAL HEALTH

ATTENTION DEFICIT HYPERACTIVITY DISORDER
Discusses symptoms, causes, diagnosis, and treatments of this disorder which affects many children and young people. 42 pp. **#330D. 50¢.**

ANXIETY DISORDERS
Treatments available and resources to contact for more information on panic phobias, stress, obsessive-compulsive, and other anxiety disorders. 24 pp. **#567D. Free.**

BIPOLAR DISORDER (MANIC-DEPRESSIVE ILLNESS)
Learn signs and symptoms, available treatments, and how to get help. 12 pp. **# 568D. Free.**

EATING DISORDERS
Both overeating and excessive dieting can be life-threatening illnesses. Learn symptoms, possible medical complications, treatments, how to help, and resources for more information. 17 pp **#.376D. 50¢.**

HELPING THE DEPRESSED PERSON GET TREATMENT
Gives specific advice and examples of symptoms, and treatments to help. 23 pp. **# 569D. Free.**

MEDICATIONS FOR THE TREATMENT OF SCHIZOPHRENIA
Questions and Answers. Describes various medications and how they work, gives a range of usual daily doses and discusses side effects. 13 pp. **#570D Free.**

OBSESSIVE-COMPULSIVE DISORDER
Learn how to identify, treat, and get help for excessively repetitive thoughts and behaviors that are distressing and extremely difficult to overcome. 16 pp. . **#571D. Free.**

PANIC DISORDER
What to do when anxiety or sudden fear seems too much to handle. Lists symptoms, treatments, and where to get help. 2 pp. **# 572D. Free.**

PLAIN TALK ABOUT DEPRESSION
Depression has many symptoms. Learn how it's diagnosed, treated, and how to get help. 4 pp. **# 573D. Free.**

HOUSING · BUYING & FINANCING

CONSUMER HANDBOOK ON ADJUSTABLE RATE MORTGAGES.
Describes basic features, advantages, risks, and terminology. Explains how ARM's work and how to reduce your risks. 25 pp. **#331D. 50¢.**

A CONSUMER'S GUIDE TO MORTGAGE LOCK-INS
Lists questions to ask when shopping for a mortgage. 14 pp. **# 332D. 50¢.**

A CONSUMER'S GUIDE TO MORTGAGE REFINANCINGS
Is refinancing beneficial for you? Learn the costs, and how to tell if the time is right. 8 pp. **#333D. 50¢.**

ENERGY EFFICIENT MORTGAGE HOME OWNER GUIDE
If you're buying, refinancing, or remodeling, you could increase your comfort and save money with a mortgage that covers energy-saving repairs. 9 pp. **# 609D. Free**

HOME BUYER'S VOCABULARY
Defines common words and terms used in the real estate world. Especially useful for the first time buyer. 14 pp. **#121D. $1.00.**

THE HOME INSPECTION & YOU
Answers questions about how and why you should get a home inspection before buying or selling. 2 pp. **#334D. 50¢.**

HOW TO BUY A HOME WITH A LOW DOWN PAYMENT
There are private and federal options for obtaining a mortgage. Learn how to qualify, determine what you can afford, and more. 12 pp. **# 574D. Free.**

HOW TO BUY A MANUFACTURED (MOBILE) HOME
Tips on selection and placement, warranties, site preparation, transportation, installation, and more. 22 pp. **#377D. 50¢.**

THE HUD HOMEBUYING GUIDE
Here are step-by-step instructions for finding and financing a HUD home. Includes charts to help you estimate mortgage payments. 11 pp. **#575D. Free.**

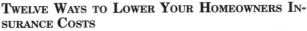

TWELVE WAYS TO LOWER YOUR HOMEOWNERS INSURANCE COSTS
Practical tips to help reduce your expenses. Lists phone numbers of state insurance departments for more information. 4 pp. **#335D. 50¢.**

HOME IMPROVEMENTS & SAFETY

BACKYARD BIRD PROBLEMS
How to control common problems such as destruction of garden plants, nesting in gutters and chimneys, and damage to your home's exterior. 27 pp. **#576D. Free.**

FIXING UP YOUR HOME AND HOW TO FINANCE IT
Basic information about hiring a contractor, doing the work yourself, and the Title 1 loan program (a loan for making home improvements). 2 pp **#378D. 50¢.**

A HOME ELECTRICAL SAFETY CHECK
Lists sumptoms of potential electrical hazards, discusses do's and don'ts, and poses questions to help you keep your home safe. 17 pp. **#337D. 50¢.**

HOME WATER TREATMENT UNITS
Discusses various options for purifying drinking water, factors to consider before purchasing a unit, and how to avoid deceptive sales pitches. 2 pp. **#338D. 50¢.**

NEVER SAY NEVER
90% of all U.S. natural disasters involve flooding. Learn how to obtain the insurance coverage you need. 5 pp.**#577. Free**

PROTECT YOUR FAMILY FROM LEAD IN YOUR HOME
Ingesting lead is dangerous, especially to young children. Learn how to check your home and reduce the hazards. 15 pp. **#578D. Free.**

REHAB A HOME WITH HUD's 203(K)
Learn how you might get a long-term mortgage that includes the costs of reconstructing, modernizing and eliminating health and safety hazards in your home. 35 pp. **#339D. 50¢.**

REPAIRING YOUR FLOODED HOME
Step-by-step advice on cleaning up and repairing your home and its contents after a flood and how to protect your home in the future. 56 pp. **#579D. Free.**

SELECTING A NEW WATER HEATER
Describes how different types of water heaters work and features to consider when buying. 6 pp. **#122D. $1.00.**

MONEY

AT-HOME SHOPPING RIGHTS
How to deal with late deliveries, unordered merchandise, billing errors and much more when making purchases by mail or phone order. 2 pp. **#366D. 50¢.**

BANKRUPTCY
Explains what bankruptcy is, lists the different types, and what the differences mean to you in the short and long term. 5 pp. **#580D. Free.**

BEING AN EXECUTOR
Explains what an executor is and does in order to settle an estate. Includes a checklist and resources for more help if you are named an executor. 8 pp. **#581D. Free.**

BEING SUED
Describes what happens when you're sued; when to consider hiring a lawyer; and options for avoiding litigation. 10 pp. **#604D. Free.**

CYBERSHOPPING
The pros and cons of shopping on the Internet with special tips on protecting the security of a financial transaction. 2 pp. **#341D. 50¢.**

DOING YOUR TAXES
Explains what tax forms to use, how to fill them out, where to send your return, and how to get free help. Lists the most common errors to watch for. 12 pp. **#582D. Free.**

AN IRS AUDIT
Explains what an audit is, and factors that may trigger one. Here's advice that includes how to appeal the results. 8 pp. **#583D. Free.**

MAKING A WILL
Explains why a will is important, how to prepare one, what to include, and how to keep it current. 12 pp. **#584D. Free.**

MAKING SENSE OF SAVINGS
How to compare different banking accounts. De-

scribes the various services and fees, and questions to ask about interest rates and service charges. 12 pp. **#343D. 50¢**

SHOPPING WITH YOUR ATM CARD
Describes the new ways you can use an ATM card. Provides safety precautions and a listing of networks and affiliated shopping services by state. 23 pp. **#585D. Free.**

SWINDLERS ARE CALLING
Eight things you should know about telemarketing fraud, nine tip-offs that a caller could be a crook, and ten ways to avoid becoming a victim. 4 pp.**#369D. 50¢.**

CREDIT

CONSUMER HANDBOOK TO CREDIT PROTECTION LAWS
Explains how consumer credit laws can help you apply for credit, keep up a good credit standing, and complain about an unfair deal. 44 pp **#345D. 50¢.**

FAIR DEBT COLLECTION
Describes what debt collectors may and may not do if you owe money. How and where to complain if you are harassed, threatened, or abused. 2 pp. **#346D. 50¢.**

HOW TO DISPUTE CREDIT REPORT ERRORS
Gives tips on correcting errors, registering a dispute, and adding information to your file. 2 pp. **#347D. 50¢.**

MANAGING YOUR DEBTS
How to Regain Financial Health. Learn where to begin - what you can do for yourself, how counseling can help, facts about bankruptcy, and more. 2 pp. **#348D. 50¢.**

READY, SET...CREDIT
How to check your credit record and establish a good history. What to do if your credit card is lost, stolen, or turned down. 2 pp. (1996. **#349D. 50¢.**

SHOP...THE CARD YOU PICK CAN SAVE YOU MONEY
Charts 149 credit card plans to help you compare annual percentage rates, calculate finance charges, types of pricing, grace periods, and annual fees.18 pp. **#350D. 50¢.**

FINANCIAL PLANNING

ANNUITIES
Detailed information on the different types of an-

nuities that can accumulate and generate retirement income. Includes a helpful quiz and questions to ask before you purchase. 11 pp. **#586D. Free.**

66 WAYS TO SAVE MONEY
Practical ways to cut everyday costs on transportation, insurance, banking, credit, housing, utilities, food, and much more. 4 pp. **#351D. 50¢.**

BUYING TREASURY SECURITIES
Learn all about bills, notes, and bonds including purchase, payment, reinvestment, and taxation. 36 pp.# **587D. Free.**

ESTABLISHING A TRUST FUND
Explains the different types of trusts, their benefits, and gives examples of when each type is most useful. 10 pp. **#589D. Free.**

FACTS ABOUT FINANCIAL PLANNERS
What they can and can't do, what credentials to ask for, and what to expect. Includes charts for organizing your records. 12 pp. **#352D. 50¢.**

AN INTRODUCTION TO MUTUAL FUNDS
Explains what they are, how to compare them, what factors to consider before investing, and how to avoid common pitfalls. 15 pp. **#353D. 50¢.**

INVEST WISELY
Basic tips to help you select a brokerage firm and representative, make and monitor an investment, questions to ask, and signs of problems. 14 pp.**#354D. 50¢.**

INVESTMENT SWINDLES
How They Work and How To Avoid Them. Protect against illegal, yet legitimate-sounding, telemarketing and direct mail offers. Explains who swindlers are and techniques commonly used. 22 pp. **#590D. Free.**

INVESTORS' BILL OF RIGHTS
Tips to help you make an informed decision when making investments. 7 pp. **#591D. Free.**

PLANNING YOUR ESTATE
How to estimate the size of your estate; minimize taxation, and provide for your heirs. 10 pp. **#593D. Free.**

STAYING INDEPENDENT: PLANNING FOR FINANCIAL INDEPENDENCE IN LATER LIFE
Helps you evaluate your present financial status

and determine if changes are necessary. 7 pp. **#355D. 50¢.**

TOP 10 WAYS TO BEAT THE CLOCK AND PREPARE FOR RETIREMENT
Gives practical tips to help build your retirement savings, and resources for more information. 2 pp. **#594D. Free.**

UNDERSTANDING OPPORTUNITIES AND RISKS IN FUTURES TRADING
Explains the commodities market, regulations and risks involved. Discusses what to look for in a futures contract, explains terms and so much more. 46 pp. **#356D. 50¢.**

U.S. SAVINGS BONDS INVESTOR INFORMATION
Detailed information on savings bond purchase, interest, maturity, replacement, redemption, exchange, and taxes. 10 pp. **#357D. 50¢.**

VIATICAL SETTLEMENTS
Discusses options for selling your life insurance policy if you have a terminal illness, including lump sum payments, loans, and accelerated benefits. 7 pp. **#358D. 50¢.**

WHAT YOU SHOULD KNOW ABOUT BUYING LIFE INSURANCE
Describes various types with tips on choosing a company and agent, and making sure a policy meets your needs. 23 pp. **#595D. Free.**

SMALL BUSINESS

AMERICANS WITH DISABILITIES ACT
Guide for Small Businesses. Basic requirements for small businesses to ensure that their facilities are accessible. Discusses tax credits and deductions with toll-free sources for more help. 15 pp. **#620D. Free.**

GUIDE TO BUSINESS CREDIT FOR WOMEN
Minorities, and Small Businesses. Explains the preparation and application process to obtain commercial credit. 12 pp. **#360D. 50¢.**

RESOURCE DIRECTORY FOR SMALL BUSINESS MANAGEMENT.
Lists publications and video tapes useful for starting and managing a successful small business. 5 pp. **#361D. 50¢.**

RUNNING A SMALL BUSINESS
Discusses sales and marketing, record keeping,

finding advisors, partners, personnel, patents, trademarks, copyrights, financial concerns and much more. 11 pp. **#597D. Free.**

SELLING A BUSINESS
How to find a buyer, work with a broker, assess what your business is worth, handle your customer list, and finance the sale. 12 pp. **#598D. Free.**

STARTING A BUSINESS
Lists questions to ask about yourself and your business plans before you get started, discusses financing, and explains the four types of business ownership. 10 pp.**#599D. Free.**

TRAVEL & HOBBIES

DISCOVER AMERICA
A Listing of State Tourism Offices of the U. S. Use this list to order free vacation information including maps, calendars of events, travel guides, and more. 4 pp. **#379D. 50¢.**

FLY SMART.
Lists more than 30 things you can do to help make your flight a safe one. Includes a passenger checklist. 2 pp. **#600D. Free.**

FOR THE BIRDS
Three separate booklets describe how to attract different species of birds, feed them, and build or buy suitable homes. **#362D. 50¢.**

FOREIGN ENTRY REQUIREMENTS.
Lists 230 embassies and consulate addresses and phone numbers where passports and visas may be obtained. 20 pp. **#363D. 50¢.**

NEW HORIZONS FOR THE AIR TRAVELER WITH A DISABILITY
Describes accommodations, facilities, and services that are required to be available and accessible. 33 pp. **#601D. Free.**

PASSPORTS: APPLYING FOR THEM THE EASY WAY
How, when, and where to apply for U.S. passports. Includes information on fees. 2 pp. **#364D. 50¢.**

MISCELLANEOUS

ANTITRUST ENFORCEMENT AND THE CONSUMER
Revised. Explains how laws governing business

competition are enforced and how consumers benefit. 12 pp. **#621D. Free.**

A Consumer's Guide to Postal Services and Products
Describes many special mailing services that save you time and money. Revised. 40 pp. **# 605D. Free.**

1997 Consumer's Resource Handbook
Lists contacts to help with consumer problems and complaints. Includes corporate consumer representatives, private resolution programs, automobile manufacturers, government agencies, how to write an effective complaint letter and much more. 127 pp. **#623D. Free.**

Dealing with a Disability
Discusses options for housing, health care, financial benefits, work, and legal rights. Offers advice for families and friends, including sources of assistance. 12 pp.**# 603D. Free.**

Enjoying Retirement.
Lists items to think about and plan before retirement, including: daily activities, exercise, diet, finances, and more. 10 pp.**# 606D. Free.**

Funerals
A Consumer Guide. Tells what costs and services a funeral provider is required to give you when you inquire in person or by phone. 4 pp.**#367D. 50¢.**

A Guide to Disability Rights Laws
Describes your rights regarding fair housing, public accommodations, telecommunications, education and employment. 14 pp. **#622D. Free.**

Taking Legal Action
Discusses when legal action may be appropriate, how to file in small claims court, and when to consider hiring a lawyer. 10 pp. **#607D. Free.**

The U.S. and the Metric System
Everything you need to know to use metric in everyday life. Includes metric conversion charts, a cookie recipe in metric, and more. 10 pp. **#370D. 50¢.**

Your Family Disaster Supplies Kit
Lists how much and what kinds of food, first aid supplies, clothing, tools, and sanitation supplies you should

stock to care for your family in an emergency. 4 pp. **#371D. 50¢.**

U.S. GOVERNMENT TTY DIRECTOR
Phone numbers of agencies and congressional offices with Teletypewriters. These are communication devises used by individuals who are deaf, hard of hearing, and speech impared. 79 pp. **#608D. Free.**

ORDERING FREE BOOKLETS

While there is no charge for individual free publications, there is a $1.00 service fee to help defray program costs. For that $1.00, you may order up to 25 different free booklets. Payment can be made by check or money order made payable to the "Superintendent of Documents"

If you order ONLY free booklets, mail your order to:
S. JAMES
CONSUMER INFORMATION CENTER - 7B
P.O. BOX 100
PUEBLO, COLORADO 81002

If you order BOTH sales and free, or ONLY sales booklets, mail your order to:
R. WOODS
CONSUMER INFORMATION CENTER - 7B
P.O. BOX 100
PUEBLO, COLORADO 81002

Booklets listed are also available online, along with other consumer news, updates, and information. Use your modem or Internet connection to access this information electronically.

Internet World Wide Web - Electronic BBS:
http://www.pueblo.gsa.gov

Free Groceries & Gifts

- Recently a woman walked out of a Safeway supermarket in Los Angeles with over $67 in groceries without paying for them. Shoplifting? No - it was all perfectly legal

- A woman in Brewster, N.Y. bought $80 in groceries. She paid 32 cents!

- A Yonkers, N.Y. woman bought over $130 worth of food and groceries. Her total cost was only $7.07.

- A New Jersey housewife purchased $32. worth of groceries. She handed over $3.00 to the cashier.

These women make it a habit to coupon their way to hundreds...even thousands...of dollars every year in free groceries. These super-shoppers have learned to stretch the buying power of every dollar they spend.

They take advantage of the fact that many food and drug manufacturers are anxious to pay you for trying their products. These companies offer you cash refunds, free product coupons, toys and gifts of all kinds.

Here are some tips that will help you save up to $2,000 every year on your grocery bill:

1. Buy only brand name items (not store brands or no-frills). It's only on brand name products that you will get the refund checks, coupons for free products and other free gifts offered by various manufacturers. For example, when Tide is offering Timex watches as a premium you buy Tide.

2. Look for supermarkets that double the value of coupons - many supermarkets will give you $1.00 off, for example, when you give them a 50 cents coupon.

3. Save parts of the packaging for future refunds and gifts. Companies will pay cash for certain parts of their packages (like boxtops and proof of purchase seals) as proof you purchased their products.

4. Carefully check supermarket circulars and newspaper ads for extra money- saving specials. Often you can combine these spe-

cial sale prices with your coupons for a double- barrelled saving.

5. Quantity buying of specials. When your supermarket offers an extra special bargain buy more than you need right away. The more you buy the more you save.

6. Subscribe to a good refund magazine. A typical issue may contain between $100 and $200 in refund offers from hundreds of companies.

But coupons and refunds are just a part of the dollar stretcher system. A true super shopper is someone who refuses to pay more than they have to for anything they buy. But most people simply don't realize just how much their money can buy. For that reason we suggest you read the Dollar Stretcher Report.

Discover how to buy everything from film to furniture at 30% to 89% below retail. Learn how you can save hundreds of dollars on your utility bill, phone bill, car purchases, vacations. Make your savings earn the highest return and borrow money 30% -40% cheaper than the rate your bank charges.

If you'd like a copy of the Dollar Stretcher Report (including refund publications) send $2.00 for S&H to:

DOLLAR STRETCHER REPORT
Box 125 - BFT
Hartsdale, NY 10530